FORESTRY EDUCATION AT TORONTO

Members of Staff and students, Faculty of Forestry, University of Toronto 1907–8. FRONT ROW (*left to right*): T. W. Dwight, A. H. D. Ross, Dr. B. E. Fernow, E. J. Zavitz. SECOND ROW: L. M. Ellis, J. H. White, F. M. Mitchell, R. P. Wodehouse.

Forestry Education at Toronto

J. W. B. SISAM

University of Toronto Press

Copyright, Canada, 1961, by
University of Toronto Press
Printed in Canada
Reprinted in 2018
ISBN 978-1-4875-8245-6 (paper)

Foreword

THE PURPOSE of this book is to provide the Alumni of the Faculty of Forestry with some record of the history of the Faculty and of the people and events that influenced its development over the past fifty years. Its preparation was suggested by the Council of the Forestry Alumni Association at the time arrangements were being made to mark the semi-centennial anniversary of the Faculty, the intention being to have it ready for distribution in the fall of 1957. R. M. Watt, a member of the class of 1913 and for many years on the staff of the Dominion Forest Service in charge of its public relations programme, kindly undertook to write the text, but had barely commenced work on it when he suffered a heart attack and died on February 4, 1957. The present author was not able to give the project his undivided attention at the time, and as a result it has been written in bits and pieces, and its publication is long overdue.

Because of the close association there must be between training and practice in the developmental stages of an applied science, it has been necessary in discussing the history of forestry education in Ontario to make reference to many matters outside the immediate responsibility of the Faculty; in all cases, however, these are related in some degree to the work of the Faculty, either in their influence on its programme or in their being influenced by the views and extra-curricular activities of its staff.

Financial support for the publication of this work has been provided by Alumni, individually and through the Forestry Alumni Association, and by the Associates of the University of Toronto Inc., New York. To these groups and individuals, the author and Faculty are most grateful.

J.W.B.S.

Contents

Foreword		v
I	Historical Background	3
II	Establishment and Early Development 1907–19	19
III	Further Developments: The Influence of Industrial Expansion and Government Policy	33
IV	Forestry Under Low Pressure 1929–39	43
V	War and Post-War 1939–60	49
VI	Curriculum, Enrolment, and Employment	60
VII	Graduate Studies and Research	72
VIII	University Forest and Ranger School	78
IX	Undergraduate and Alumni Affairs	84
Appendixes		
	I. University of Toronto, Statute Number 491	95
	II. The Enrolment of Students in the Faculty of Forestry 1907–61	96
	III. Officers of Undergraduate and Graduate Organizations	99
	IV. Original Curriculum, 1907	102
	V. Undergraduate Scholarships, Prizes, and Medals	103
	VI. Members of the Staff	105
	VII. Graduates in Forestry by Years	106
References		113

Illustrations

Staff and Students, Faculty of Forestry, 1907–8   *frontispiece*

Between pages 40 and 41

First Field Instruction Given Forestry Students in Canada, Rondeau Park, 1908

Second Annual Forestry Dinner, January 30, 1913

Gathering at the Dedication of the Forestry Building, January 21, 1926

Special Convocation, Fiftieth Anniversary, Faculty of Forestry

Members of Staff and Alumni, Faculty of Forestry, 1960

Faculty of Forestry Football Team, 1950

Faculty of Forestry Basketball Team, 1930

Number 11 Queen's Park

The Forestry Building

The Ontario Forest Ranger School

Glendon Hall Botany and Forestry Laboratories and Greenhouse

Wood Technology Laboratory

FORESTRY EDUCATION AT TORONTO

I. Historical Background

There is no doubt that a great work in forestry can be done in this Province by the University, provided it receives the co-operation and encouragement of the Government (51).

ALTHOUGH IT IS just over fifty years since the first Canadian forestry school was established, the reasons for this action and the events leading up to it go well back into the history of the nineteenth century. Indeed, one might say that the situation which brought about a demand for university graduates in forestry was inherent in the country when the first European settlers arrived here—a situation represented by the natural resources of the country and the problems and opportunities associated with their use and development.

To the early settlers and their immediate descendants, the vast primeval forests were a hazard to life and an obstacle to settlement. While the fur-bearing animals that inhabited them provided the basis for the country's first major industry, the timber itself was for many years of little direct value; the potential wealth these forests represented could only be realized as the country was opened up and markets for their products developed. As settlement began, and for many years afterwards, it was the general feeling that the forest must be removed, the sooner the better, in order to extend the area available for agriculture. Something of this view is expressed in the charter of the Royal Canadian Institute (6) granted in 1851, where the objectives include those of encouraging and promoting "the arts of opening up the wilderness and preparing the country for the pursuits of the agriculturists . . . and otherwise smoothing the path of civilization." Even as late as the 1890's, Ontario was regarded by many as "a purely agricultural country, adapted only to agriculture, in which timber was not considered a profitable crop" (22, p. 6); this despite the fact that for a period of some seventy-five years the wood-using industries had been growing in size, becoming more diversified, and making an increasingly important contribution to the economic development of the country. It should be added that this was not a view supported by the agricultural scientists, many of whom were among the early advocates of forest conservation and reforestation.

The forests began to play an important part in Canadian commerce during the first quarter of the nineteenth century, when the export of square timbers to Great Britain increased rapidly as a result of Napoleon's blockade of northwest Europe and the British Government's preferential treatment of imports from the North American colonies. During the second half of the century, the export trade in forest products changed in kind and direction and increased in volume in response to the growing demand in the United States for sawn lumber to meet the needs of a rapidly expanding population, particularly on the Atlantic seaboard. This was soon to be followed by a demand for wood as the raw material for a new industry—pulp, paper, and paper products—which in the course of time would be the means of opening the northern forests of Canada to commercial enterprise.

Thus the forests of the country came under pressure from two directions, on the one hand to clear land as quickly as possible for settlement, and on the other to supply a rapidly increasing demand for lumber and other wood products. Up to a point, these were both highly desirable and indeed essential activities for the proper growth and development of the country, but beyond this point they inevitably led to problems and difficulties which only gradually came to be recognized, and some of which would require specialized knowledge for their solution.

Forest fires, whether of natural or human origin, were common in lumbering and land-clearing operations; indeed in the early days much of the hardwood timber removed to make way for settlement was burned for lack of a market. As a result, large volumes of timber were destroyed, and often the growth capacity of the land was impaired owing to the burning of organic material and the exposure and subsequent erosion of the surface soil. By the middle of the nineteenth century, with markets for timber products expanding, the fire problem began to receive attention, at least from some lumbermen who recognized that frequent and severe fires could only have an adverse effect on the future prosperity of their industry. Although the authority of provincial governments in eastern Canada with respect to the

HISTORICAL BACKGROUND 5

public lands and forests within their boundaries was established by the Act of Confederation (1867),[1] it was only after persistent effort by a few men, who realized the seriousness of the situation, that the first legislative action in the matter of forest fire protection was taken in Ontario, when the Government in 1878 passed a statute entitled "An Act to Preserve the Forests from Destruction by Fire." Seven years later, in 1885, as the result of a memorandum submitted by Mr. Aubrey White[2] to the Commissioner of Crown Lands, a fire-ranging system was organized; this was the beginning of what would eventually become one of the largest and most effective forest protection organizations in existence.

Concurrent with the early concern with fire protection was the realization, again by only a few people, first, that much of the land being cleared of timber was not suited to the growing of agricultural crops, second, that the forest was a valuable resource, and third, that certain types of land could best be used for the continuous production of timber. It was also apparent that at the rate forest land was being cleared the valuable pine forests would soon be exhausted. Thus in his report of 1864–5, the Commissioner of Crown Lands, the Honourable Alexander Campbell, stated (22, p. 96):

Should the whole of our uncultivatable lands be set apart, as I think should be done, as a pine region, and no sales made there, the land would, if the trees were cut under a system of rotation such as is now adopted in Norway and Sweden and in many of the German states, recuperate their growth of merchantable pine in cycles of thirty and forty years, and pine growing might be continued and preserved for ages to come. In view of the future requirements of this continent and of Europe, and of the singular advantages Canada enjoys as a pine-producing country, I humbly submit that it is of the utmost importance that we should now take steps in this direction.

Again, a publication entitled *The Lumber Trade of the Ottawa Valley*[3] called for conservation of the forest and advocated the establishment of tree nurseries for the perpetuation of the pine species.

---

[1]Under subsection 5 of section 92 of the British North America Act, the provinces were given full jurisdiction over "the management and sale of public lands and the timber and wood thereon."

[2]At that time Chief Clerk of the Woods and Forests Branch of the Crown Lands Department. See 22, pp. 130–3.

[3]Published by the Times Printing and Publishing Co., Ottawa, 1872, 3rd edition.

Twenty years later, in 1893, Algonquin Park was set aside as a game and timber preserve (22, pp. 125, 138), and in 1897 a Royal Commission was appointed to investigate the situation with respect to white pine resources in the Province of Ontario. The recommendations of this Commission led in the following year to the passing of the Forest Reserves Act, the implementation of which resulted in the withdrawal from settlement of 16,395 square miles of forest (60). It was pointed out at the time that this Act, in providing for perpetual government ownership of a large area of forest land, constituted the initial step in preparing for a rational system of forest management.[4]

Other problems associated with forest exploitation and land clearance that were recognized at a fairly early stage included the tremendous waste of material resulting from lumbering operations[5] and the need to re-establish tree vegetation on denuded areas, especially for the purpose of protecting farm land and the sources of water supply.[6]

Similar problems were being discussed in the United States and elsewhere in Canada, and gradually more people in both countries came to be interested in forestry matters, and through the associations they formed, the meetings they held, and the publications they issued, the idea of forest conservation began to be accepted and promoted.

Thus a conservation movement, based largely on the needs of forestry, began in the United States about the middle of the nineteenth century and soon had repercussions in this country. An early

[4]Prior to this, retention by the Crown of the bulk of the land area of the Province was not associated in the minds of government with forest conservation, but rather with efforts to ensure orderly settlement of the land and maximum revenue to the Crown.

[5]Thomas Southworth, after a number of years as Director of Forestry in Ontario, stated in 1907 that he very much doubted "if there is any other business in this country carried on with so little regard for economy, with so much waste, as the great lumber industry" (59, p. 299).

[6]In 1871 and again in 1883, legislation was passed by the Ontario Government to encourage tree planting, mainly on highways and boundary lines. While these acts were ineffective and later repealed, the authority for government assistance in tree planting for these purposes has been maintained in a succession of acts and amendments thereof, the authority at present being under the Municipal Act, R.S.O., 1950, c. 243, s. 483, and the Highway Improvement Act, 1957, 5–6 Eliz. II, c. 43, s. 29(4).

A more direct approach to land reclamation was first undertaken by the Department of Agriculture in 1903 when a forest nursery was established at the Ontario Agricultural College and subsequently planting stock was distributed to farmers free of charge for use in afforesting waste land. The main purpose was educational, i.e., to have representative plantations distributed throughout the Province to demonstrate what could be done along these lines.

meeting of special significance was that of the American Forestry Congress held in Cincinnati, Ohio, in 1882, as it was there that the first permanent forestry organization in North America came into being (53, p. 51 *et seq.*). This meeting was attended by a number of Canadian delegates, including three from Ontario—Mr. William Saunders, Director of the Dominion Experimental Farm at Ottawa, Mr. D. W. Beadle, a prominent nurseryman from St. Catharines, and Professor William Brown of the Ontario Agricultural College. Thus we see that agriculture was well represented by those taking an early interest in forestry in this Province, though it is probable that this interest was more closely associated with the protection and amelioration of farm lands by forest plantings than with the management of forest lands as such.

At the invitation of the Canadian delegates, the Congress was re-convened in Montreal in August of the same year (1882). Prominent among the Canadian leaders at that meeting were Mr. William Little of Montreal and Sir Henri Joly de Lotbinière of Quebec.

At the meetings in both Cincinnati and Montreal, an outstanding impression was made by a young man, Bernard Eduard Fernow by name, who at the time was the only professionally educated forester in North America. Born in Posen, Prussia, in 1851, Fernow had studied under Heyer and other famous German foresters. He had come to the United States from Germany in 1876, and over the course of the next forty-five years was to exert a tremendous influence on forestry development—technical, administrative, and educational—in both the United States and Canada. In 1886, he became the first Chief of the Division of Forestry in the Department of Agriculture at Washington; in 1898, he established the first professional forestry school in the United States at Cornell University; and in 1907, he became the first Dean of the Faculty of Forestry, University of Toronto.

One result of the Montreal meeting of the Congress was the establishment in 1883 of the position of Clerk of Forestry by the Ontario Government mainly for the purpose of informing the public on forestry matters; Mr. Robert W. Phipps was first appointed to this post, which during his tenure of office was attached to the Department of Agriculture. Mr. Phipps' extensive reports emphasized among other things the problems arising from settlement of lands unfit for agriculture, the value in reforesting these lands, and the need for better fire protection and "conservative management" of the remaining forests. In 1895 the forestry office was transferred to the Department of Crown Lands, and Mr. Thomas Southworth, who succeeded Mr. Phipps as Clerk of Forestry, was directed to study "the situation on the lands of the Crown, to ascertain what was best to be done in the way of reforesting the cut and burned-over areas of Crown lands, not suited for farming, as well as to suggest improvements in the handling of the timber on the Crown domain" (58). Mr. Southworth, who later was Director of Forestry for the Province, became a strong advocate of the establishment of a school for the training of professional foresters.

While the Forestry Congress of 1882 was international in character, with Canadian representatives taking an active part, and although Canadians attended subsequent meetings of the Congress and the American Forestry Association (as it later became), there was only one further meeting held in Canada, that being in Quebec in 1890. In the years to follow, the activities of the American Forestry Association had little influence on public opinion in this country.

In January, 1900, Mr. Elihu Stewart, who had recently been appointed Chief Inspector of Timber and Forestry for the Dominion Government, called together a group of interested men to consider the formation of an association for the purpose of promoting forestry in Canada. As a result, the Canadian Forestry Association was formed, the first meeting being held in Ottawa on March 8, 1900, with Sir Henri Joly de Lotbinière as Chairman (48). The primary object of this association was to inform the general public of the value of the forest resource and the importance of its protection against fire and other destructive agencies.

At the first and subsequent annual meetings of the Association, attended by members from all parts of the country, papers were presented on a wide range of subjects relating to Canada's forests, including accounts of forest conditions and problems of forest administration in the different provinces and territories, forest fire losses (the most serious single problem) and means for fire control, the establishment of shelterbelts in the Prairie Provinces, the maintenance of forest cover to protect water resources, and a great many other matters of interest and importance. While much of value came out of these papers and discussions, it was frequently pointed out by those in attendance that they were only able to consider the problems in a rather general way and that ultimately the development and management of the forest resource would depend on having men properly trained to study them on a scientific basis. This view was expressed by Mr. Southworth at the third annual meeting of the Association in March, 1902, as follows:

Whatever plan may be adopted for disposing of this timber [in the Temagami Reserve], it is evident to thoughtful men that the time has arrived when we need more highly trained men in our forests than are now available in any considerable number. So long as lumbering was considered an ephemeral business and not a permanent industry, the need of scientifically trained men was not so apparent as now, and I believe the need will not only be appreciated generally in a short time, but will be supplied. (57)

In the meantime and preceding the formation of the Canadian Forestry Association, a considerable interest in professional forestry education in this country had been stimulated as a result of an address given by Dr. Fernow[7] at a public meeting of the Royal Society of Canada in 1894 (43). Among those present was Dr. W. L. Goodwin, Director of the School of Mining at Queen's University, who from that time became interested in the possibility of introducing a forestry course at that institution, and in the following winter suggested to the Senate that Dr. Fernow be invited to give a series of lectures. This was not possible at the time. However, during 1896 and the years following, Dr. Goodwin and Dr. Fernow carried on an exchange of letters discussing the means whereby forestry might be combined with instruction in geology, engineering, and economics, and a system established for the practical demonstration of the principles of forestry.

Interest was maintained, and early in 1900 the Board of Governors of the School of Mining and Agriculture at Queen's invited Dr. Fernow to Kingston to lecture and take part in a conference during January, 1901, the purpose of the conference being to consider "the best means for the preservation and renewal of our forests, for using them to the best advantage, and for providing proper education to these ends" (29, p. 2). Dr. Fernow's illustrated lecture was entitled *The Forest, Its Care, Its Use, Its Enemies, Its Management, and Reproduction.*

[7]At that time Chief of the United States Division of Forestry.

Among those attending the conference, in addition to representatives of the University, were the Honourable Mr. Harcourt, Minister of Education; Hiram Calvin, M.P.; S. Russell, M.P.P.; W. R. Dempsey, M.P.P.; E. J. B. Pense, M.P.P.; Dr. Fletcher, Dominion Entomologist; and R. H. Campbell of the Department of the Interior. In moving a vote of thanks to the lecturer, Mr. Pense pointed out that "Queen's had several branches of education not to be found at Toronto or Montreal and it would be quite in order to add another—forestry" (29, p. 3).

Many other people in responsible positions, who were unable to attend the conference, indicated by letter their strong sympathy with the idea of establishing a school of forestry in Kingston. To provide for practical field training in connection with such a school, it was suggested by Dr. A. T. Drummond (12), that the Eastern Ontario Forest Reserve within sixty miles of Kingston be made available by the Ontario Government.

While the University authorities in general supported the idea of providing for forestry instruction, it was felt that perhaps in the first place lectures on the subject should be given throughout the country in order to gain wider public support for the undertaking. This problem of providing for a more general knowledge of forestry, and associated with it that of attracting young men into the profession, was discussed by Dr. Goodwin in the *Queen's Quarterly* (25) on the basis of experience in mining engineering a few years earlier; Dr. Goodwin suggested that in forestry a start be made by providing (*a*) short introductory courses during the winter for practical men already engaged in forestry work, (*b*) summer field courses for those interested in making a career in this field, and (*c*) scholarships and fellowships to support suitable candidates unable to finance a university education.

In the meantime, arrangements were made for Dr. Fernow to deliver a further series of lectures in Kingston, in January, 1903, these to be considered preliminary and introductory to the beginning of the school of forestry in the following session. Under the sanction of the Board of Governors of that university, these lectures were published (19) and given wide distribution.[8]

---

[8]These lectures include the following subjects: "The Forest as a Resource," "What is Forestry?", "How Trees Grow," "The Evolution of a Forest Growth," "Silviculture or Methods of Forest Crop Production," "Lumbermen and Forester,"

HISTORICAL BACKGROUND 11

In a paper presented by Dr. Goodwin before the Canadian Forestry Association in March of that year (26), he stated:

... this course [of lectures] attracted a good deal of attention, and the interest in forestry seems now to be widespread. ... one result ... has been to determine several of our students to make forestry their profession. In order to do this, they must complete a course of study; and our Board of Governors have determined to go forward next session as far as circumstances will permit them to make provision for such a course of study. The wherewithal is the only puzzling circumstance.

In this connection it may be noted that, following Dr. Fernow's lectures in January, 1903, the Honourable William Harty, Chairman of the Board of Governors of the School of Mining and Agriculture, was able to say that the Premier of the Province had promised a grant of money to assist in the establishment of a school of forestry as soon as the necessary building was ready[9] and that by the date of writing (January 15, 1903) the building had been completed (29). In conclusion Mr. Harty stated that "During this whole period no other Canadian university or school of practical science has, so far as known, taken any active measures to establish a school of forestry."

This view was contradicted, however, two months later when, in commenting on the paper given by Dr. Goodwin before the Canadian Forestry Association, Mr. J. H. Faull[10] of the University of Toronto pointed out that forestry education had been under discussion at that institution for the past two years,[11] although it was "only within the

---

"Forest Economy or Business Methods," "Wood and its Characteristics," "Forest Policy," and "The Forester an Engineer." The lectures were reprinted in 1957 by the Department of Lands and Forests, Toronto.

[9]In legislation entitled "An Act to amend the Act respecting the School of Mining and Agriculture at Kingston," which received assent on April 15, 1901, it was stated explicitly that "The said corporation is hereby authorized and empowered to establish and maintain classes for the training and education of students in electrical science, optics, forestry, and all branches of biological, geological, and physical science" (29, p. 5).

[10]Lecturer in Botany who subsequently gave the course in forest pathology to forestry students at Toronto for a number of years, and became Head of the Department of Botany in 1918.

[11]It may be noted that on February 13, 1903, Professor I. H. Cameron brought to the attention of the Senate of the University of Toronto certain statements which appeared in the News of February 12 with reference to instruction in forestry at Queen's University. On his motion, the Senate agreed that a deputation should wait upon the Premier and the Minister of Education and urge action towards the establishment of the School of Forestry at Toronto.

last year that the matter has taken something like definite shape" (26, p. 92). Mr. Faull went on to say that the course planned for the University of Toronto was to be of three years' duration and that he could list the subjects it was proposed to give in each year of the course.

The interest of the University of Toronto in forestry education was confirmed and described in some detail the following year (March, 1904), when the President, James Loudon, addressed the Canadian Forestry Association at its fifth annual meeting held in Toronto (36). At that time Dr. Loudon informed the delegates that the Senate of the University had passed a statute [see Appendix I] giving academic authority for a three-year diploma course in forestry. According to Dr. Loudon, this course was patterned in part on that being given at the Yale Forestry School which had been established in 1900.

Quite naturally the interest of the two universities in sponsoring forestry education and in seeking government support for its undertaking led to a lively discussion on the lecture platform and in the press; on one occasion the University of Toronto was accused of "sailing in like a leviathan to snatch a morsel from Queen's"—the morsel being the proposed school of forestry.

Also about this time, a lecture course in forestry was being given to the degree students (in agriculture) at the Ontario Agricultural College, and the suggestion was made on more than one occasion that the College would be interested in expanding its work in this field (33). In 1903 Mr. E. J. Zavitz, a graduate of McMaster University who had taken postgraduate work in forestry at the University of Michigan, was appointed to the College staff to give instruction in forestry and to undertake the raising of nursery stock to be distributed among Ontario farmers for planting as shelterbelts and commercial plantations on denuded agricultural land. This appointment was a natural outcome of the early interest of agriculturists in forestry problems, particularly in southern Ontario, though it may also have been influenced by Dr. Fernow through his papers on "The Evolution of the Forest" and "The Farmer's Woodlot," given before the Ontario Experimental Union in December, 1902 (17, 18). In the following year, this Union submitted to the Government of Ontario a number of resolutions with respect to forestry, the first of which strongly urged upon the Government "the necessity for establishing at the earliest possible date a school of forestry, where instruction will be given in practical methods of dealing with forestry problems" (65, p. 40).

A year later, the Canadian Forestry Association again had this matter under discussion, and it is stated in the annual report of the Board of Directors for that year that

the time seems to have arrived for a more systematic and scientific study in Canada of the conditions of reproduction and development of the forest, so that the data may be available on which to base plans of management. The public interest in the subject is growing in a gratifying manner, but in order that wise action may be taken in silvicultural operations, the information at the disposal of the authorities should be much more exact and definite than such as is now available. The Association might very well bring this matter specially to the notice of the governments, so that steps towards this end may be taken with as little delay as possible. (45, p. 10)

It was, no doubt, due partly to this and partly to the discussion on forestry education introduced by Dr. Loudon's paper that later in the meeting the Association unanimously resolved "that the Ontario Government be and is hereby requested to make an appropriate grant for the operation of a provincial school or schools of forestry" (36, p. 52).

No immediate action was taken on these and other similar recommendations, and in his presidential address at the National Forestry Convention held in Ottawa in 1906, Mr. E. G. Joly de Lotbinière[12] again expressed the hope "that before long steps may be taken to organize a Canadian forestry school, where our young men may be enabled to receive a forestry education of a character suited to the needs of our country" (47, p. 22).

In the meantime in 1905, a Royal Commission was appointed by the Ontario Government to study and report on the affairs of the University of Toronto. This commission made a very careful study as to the needs of a university department for the training of professional foresters and the requirements of such a department, if it was to be effective; members of the Commission visited various forestry schools in the United States and interviewed Dr. Fernow, who at that time was acting as a consultant forester in New York.

In their report (51), submitted to the Lieutenant-Governor in April 1906, the Commission recommended the establishment of a forestry school at Toronto in the following terms (in part):

The distinctively State character of the University entails upon it obligations in respect of all the great provincial interests in which higher education is an important factor. This is eminently true of instruction in forestry.

[12]The son of Sir Henri Joly de Lotbinière, first president of the C.F.A.

The value to the country of scientific work in forestry has been already recognized upon this continent, but in Canada little has been done to apply systematically the lessons taught equally by sound economic theory and practical experience. It is surprising that Ontario with its rich areas of timber has hitherto failed to set up a school of forestry in its own university for the double purpose of providing technical training for young men in an important branch of science and of benefiting in the conservation of its forest wealth by their knowledge and skill. It would be difficult to mention a case in which the State's duty and interest go more completely hand in hand. . . .

There is no doubt that a great work in forestry can be done in this Province by the University, provided it receives the co-operation and encouragement of the Government. The Agricultural College has already provided for instruction in agricultural forestry which meets the needs of farmers with woodlots to care for and develop. The larger problem is that which touches the immense Crown domain urgently calling for the application there of the newest discoveries in forestry and for the training of skilled men to conduct experiments on a large scale in order to test methods of reforestation and the conservation of valuable timber. . . .

. . . The possession by the Crown of timber lands, where practical instruction and experiments could be carried on, simplifies the situation, and we recommend that the closest co-operation compatible with the ends sought should exist between the University authorities and the Department of Lands. It should likewise be kept in view that the private owners of timber lands have a direct interest in the supply of trained men produced by such a school and in the results of experiments made. . . . We are strongly of the view that the people of Ontario will endorse the action of the Government in creating a school of forestry by means of which the scientific treatment of our forests can be effectively carried out.

On the basis of this endorsation and within the terms of the University of Toronto Act (1906), the Board of Governors of the University on March 28, 1907, established the Faculty of Forestry and appointed Dr. Fernow as the first Dean.[13]

[13]The following are extracts from the minutes of the meeting of the Board of Governors with respect to the establishment of the Faculty of Forestry and the appointment of Dr. Fernow as Dean:
February 14, 1907
"The President made a verbal report on behalf of the Special Committee on Forestry, and recommended that a Faculty of Forestry be established. The report was approved and the following Statute passed to create such a Faculty.
" 'Statute No. 8
" '*of the Governors of the University of Toronto*
" 'WHEREAS under and by virtue of "The University Act, 1906," the Board of Governors of the University of Toronto is empowered to establish such Faculties, Departments, Chairs, and Courses of Instruction in the University of Toronto as to the Board may seem meet;

In the meantime during the session 1906–7 a committee of the Senate had prepared a report on the proposed faculty of forestry, setting out the requirements for admission and the degrees to be offered, outlining the curriculum for a four-year undergraduate course with a short account of the subjects to be given, and discussing briefly the opportunities for graduates in this field (44). On May 13, 1907, Statute No. 585, prescribing a curriculum in forestry,[14] was passed by the University Senate, thus giving academic authority for this course to be offered in the University of Toronto.

The University, in making provision for forestry education, was commended by those who had been advocating such action. Thus the Board of Directors of the Canadian Forestry Association in their report to the ninth annual meeting, held in March 1908, stated that "the most outstanding forward step made in the forestry movement in Canada during the past year was the establishment of a Faculty of Forestry in the University of Toronto under the principalship of Dr. B. E. Fernow. Dr. Fernow is one of the best known leaders in the history of forestry in the United States, and the work of himself and his school in Canada will be watched with sympathetic interest by all those interested in Canadian forestry."(46)

That the time was ripe for such action was evidenced by the almost immediate establishment of other forestry schools, at the University of New Brunswick in 1908 and at Laval University in 1910. British Columbia, with its rapidly growing industries, established a profes-

---

" 'AND WHEREAS it has seemed to the Board desirable to establish a Faculty of Forestry;
" 'NOW THEREFORE IT IS HEREBY ENACTED by the Board of Governors of the University of Toronto:
" 'THAT pursuant to its said powers, a Faculty of Forestry in the University of Toronto be and the same is hereby established.
" 'Passed this 14th day of February, A.D. 1907.

" '(Sgd.) JOHN HOSKIN
" 'Chairman.' "

March 28, 1907
"The President reported on behalf of the Special Committee on Forestry, and read his recommendation that Professor Bernhard E. Fernow be appointed Dean of the Faculty of Forestry; which was approved by the Board, and the appointment made. On motion of Dr. Walker, the salary was fixed at thirty-five hundred dollars ($3,500.00) per annum."

[14]The Statute appears in the minutes of the Senate as follows:
"By the Senate
"Be it enacted
"That the accompanying sheets containing the prescription of Courses be the curriculum in Forestry for 1907–08 (Arts Calendar 1907–08, pages 293–300)."

sional school of forestry at its provincial university a decade later, in 1921.

The history that led to the establishment of the school at Toronto was influenced by many people, conditions, and events. In Ontario, there were men such as Thomas Southworth and Aubrey White, for many years Deputy Commissioner of Lands and Mines and the first Deputy Minister of the Department of Lands, Forests, and Mines when it was formed, who, while not professional foresters, had been responsible for considerable progress in forest administration in this Province and were strongly in favour of establishing a forestry school here. Mr. White had made the appointment in 1904 of the first provincial forester, Dr. Judson F. Clark, a graduate of the Ontario Agricultural College and Cornell University (in forestry).

Outside Ontario, it was perhaps Dr. Fernow who played the most significant part in creating and stimulating an interest in forestry among many influential people in eastern Canada. He and Dr. Drummond in particular were responsible for the important conferences and lectures on forestry and forestry education that took place at Queen's University at the turn of the century.

Undoubtedly the Canadian Forestry Association contributed more than any other group in bringing to the attention of governments and the public at large the urgent need for having professionally trained foresters in this country. Also of considerable importance was the progress in forestry education taking place in the United States, where prior to 1907 professional courses in this field had been established at no less than ten universities.

Finally, one can say that the economic climate of the first decade of the twentieth century was particularly favourable for the undertaking. The country was growing in population, and its economy was expanding; this economy had been strongly supported by the lumber industry for the past fifty years. The demand and prices for lumber were rising rapidly, while the accessible supply of pine sawtimber was shrinking. The pulp and paper industry was in its infancy, but showed signs of rapid growth, bringing with it new problems in forest administration.

That forestry had become a matter of national concern is apparent, when one remembers that in 1906 a forestry convention, held under the auspices of the Canadian Forestry Association, was called to meet at Ottawa by the Right Honourable Sir Wilfrid Laurier, Prime Minister of Canada, and was addressed by the Governor-General as well as the Prime Minister and the Leader of the Opposition (47).

In speaking before one of the technical sessions of this conference, Mr. E. J. Zavitz was able to say that "Forestry is being brought before the general public in newspaper and magazine articles as never before in the history of the country. The efforts of the Canadian Forestry Association, the general rise in wood prices, and the wonderful development of the forestry movement in the United States, has done much to awaken the people of Canada." (67)

This then was the background against which university education in forestry began in this country. While there was general interest and support for its undertaking, inevitably questions were raised as to the objectives and functions of the professional forester in relation to the very practical problems associated with the administration and operation of the forest resource. It was the view of some that the immediate aim should be intensive management of the forests similar to that practised in northern Europe, and indeed for these people this was the only justification for university work in this field. On the other hand, there were those who, recognizing the great differences between Europe and Canada in forest conditions, the *per capita* area of forests, and the standards of forest products utilization, warned that intensive management practices were impractical for this country. This was the view of Mr. Southworth, who suggested as a general prescription that the first thing to be done was to see that areas of land suitable for tree growing were reserved for that purpose, second, so to direct the cutting of standing timber as to assure a uniform and continuous harvest of the right sort of trees, and third, to keep fire out of the forest (22). These are indeed sound, basic objectives with which no one could quarrel and which are still far from being fully attained in this country.

During the first half of the twentieth century the direction and speed of forestry development have been influenced by many factors, opinions, and conditions, not the least important being the general pattern of Canada's economic development. Indeed forestry, being so newly established and closely associated with the trade and industry of the country, has been especially susceptible to the fluctuations of the economic climate during this period.

Trends and developments in forestry education have in turn been influenced by changing conditions as will be apparent in reading this account of the history of the Faculty of Forestry, University of Toronto, over the past fifty years. Of the eight chapters which follow, the first four present a chronological account of the history of the Faculty, and the last four discuss certain phases of its programme that are considered of special importance.

II. Establishment and Early Development 1907-19

The First or Pioneering Stage

THIS PERIOD of the Faculty's history coincides with Dr. Fernow's tenure of office as Dean. It began when the country was enjoying a good measure of prosperity accompanied by industrial development and large-scale immigration. Within six years, however, economic depression had set in, and this was soon to be followed by four years of war, in which Canada was to be heavily involved.

These twelve years represent the last phase of Fernow's professional career. For him, it was undoubtedly a period of further accomplishment, though intermingled with difficulties and disappointments. The war was a particularly trying time, involving as it did a conflict between his homeland and the country of his adoption.

Accomplishment began with the establishment of a new school which, largely as a result of the personal qualities of the Dean, his unbounded energy and enthusiasm for his subject and his students, soon became a vigorous and effective unit within the University. And beyond the Faculty, Dr. Fernow's leadership and technical ability were quickly recognized and in demand in the wider fields of forestry interest across the country. This in turn led to enquiries for his students and graduates to undertake technical work in different parts of Canada.

In addition to Dr. Fernow, the staff of the new Faculty in the beginning consisted of two lecturers, A. H. D. Ross and E. J. Zavitz, both of whom held master's degrees in forestry from American universities. Mr. Zavitz was appointed on a part-time basis only, being employed also with the Department of Agriculture at Guelph. In the following year he resumed full-time work with that department, and in 1912 was appointed Director of the newly established Forestry Branch within the Department of Lands, Forests, and Mines.

Mr. Ross had taught school in Ontario for a number of years after receiving his M.A. at Queen's University in 1889; in 1906 he obtained his M.F. degree at Yale, and subsequently joined the Dominion Forestry Branch where he was employed as Technical Assistant. In the fall of 1907, he was appointed to the Faculty staff as Lecturer in Mensuration, Wood Utilization, and Forest Protection.

In 1914, Mr. Ross was succeeded by W. N. Millar, who had graduated in science from the University of Pennsylvania in 1906 and received his M.F. degree from Yale in 1908; he was appointed with the rank of Assistant Professor to teach Mensuration, Logging, and Wood Utilization. At the time of his appointment, Professor Millar had just completed three years with the Dominion Forestry Branch as District Inspector of Forest Reserves in Alberta, and before that had been with the United States Forest Service in charge of the Kaniksu National Forest in Idaho. In 1917, he went on leave of absence to serve with the American Army.

In the meantime in 1909, Dr. C. D. Howe had been appointed Joint Lecturer in Forestry and Botany, and in the following year J. H. White received a similar appointment.[1] Dr. Howe, a graduate in science from the University of Vermont, with his Ph.D. degree from the University of Chicago (1904), had had three years of forestry experience with the Biltmore Estate and Forest School in North Carolina as Assistant Forester and Associate Director of the School.

James Herbert White was the first graduate of the Faculty as well as being an early appointment on the staff, and as such may be considered a pioneer in professional forestry in Canada. A Blake Scholar in mathematics and science, he obtained his Bachelor's degree in Honour Science at the University of Toronto in 1904, his M.A. in 1907, his B.Sc.F. in 1909, and his Ph.D. in forest pathology in 1919. It was as a university teacher that he was best known, but in addition to the great contribution he made to the Faculty, where he was a powerful factor in establishing and maintaining high standards of scholarship, he also did much in the development of forest administration in Ontario and, indeed, had an important and constructive influence on the profession as a whole throughout Canada.

[1]In both cases the connection with the Department of Botany was terminated in 1919. Dr. Howe was made Assistant Professor in 1913 and Associate Professor in 1918, and Dr. White received similar promotions in 1917 and 1920.

Thus by degrees the early staff of the Faculty was assembled, small in numbers, but well qualified for the task they had before them.

In addition to the heavy teaching loads they carried, these men were in constant demand for extra-curricular activities—to give public addresses, to write articles for both technical and non-technical journals, and often to act in an advisory capacity to government departments. The need for such services was particularly pressing in the early stages of a young profession, of which little was generally known.

Perhaps the most demanding of these activities during this period were those associated with the Commission of Conservation[2] which was established in 1909. From the beginning, Dr. Fernow was an active member of the Commission's forestry committee, continuing with this work until he retired. Under his direction, a thorough study was made of the forest fire problem in Canada, and a number of extensive forest surveys were undertaken in different parts of the country, in particular in Nova Scotia (1910) and the Trent Watershed in southern Ontario (1912–13). The field work for these surveys was done largely by Dr. Howe and Professor White with the assistance of forestry students. Later, in 1917–18, Dr. Howe, on behalf of the Commission, made a study of pulpwood production in Quebec.

For two years, during the sessions 1917–18 and 1918–19, Professor White was on leave of absence, working for the Ontario Government as Assistant to the Provincial Forester, a newly created position to which Mr. Zavitz had been appointed; it was largely as a result of the efforts of these two men that the present pattern of forest administration, based primarily on forest protection requirements, was brought into being.

Dean Fernow, who had his roots well established in the United States before coming to this country, continued a close association with foresters and forestry activities across the border. In 1914, he was elected President of the Society of American Foresters and held that position concurrently with the presidency of the Canadian Society

---

[2]The Commission of Conservation was established by the Dominion Government in May, 1909, "to take into consideration all questions which may be brought to its notice relating to the conservation and better utilization of the natural resources of Canada, to make such inventories, collect and disseminate such information, conduct such investigations inside and outside of Canada, and frame such recommendations as seem conducive to the accomplishment of that end" (5).

of Forest Engineers.³ He had founded the American *Forestry Quarterly*, and was its editor from the beginning; when in 1917 this journal was combined with the *Proceedings of the Society of American Foresters* to become the *Journal of Forestry*, he continued as editor of the new publication.

Dr. Fernow was also interested and took an active part in the work of the Canadian Forestry Association, and became a member of the Board of Directors in 1909.

With the forestry school established, the next important problem was to find a market for its product, the university-trained forester. In the report of the Senate Committee on the Faculty of Forestry (1907) (44), it was pointed out that as forestry was hardly established on this continent, there were few known openings for graduates, but from history in other countries and of other lines of work, "the existence of a specially educated class creates a demand for their employment." Certainly at that time the professional forester was almost unknown, there being not more than ten or twelve in the whole country. Furthermore, although there had been strong support from some quarters for a forestry school, elsewhere questions were raised as to the need for young men to have a university education in order to deal with the practical problems of the forest. In the view of lumbermen, practical ability, mainly in solving problems of timber extraction, was the principal requirement for a successful woodsman. Thus in reply to an enquiry which Thomas Southworth addressed to leading lumbermen in Ontario in 1903 as to their willingness to employ forestry graduates, they were almost unanimous in the view that such graduates "would be of little use to them owing to their want of practical knowledge in the bush, sawmill, and lumber yard" (59).

³The Canadian Society of Forest Engineers (renamed the Canadian Institute of Forestry and incorporated in 1950), the national society of professional foresters, was formed on March 13, 1908, in Montreal following an annual meeting of the Canadian Forestry Association. Dr. Fernow was elected its first president. Those attending this first meeting of the Society, in addition to Dr. Fernow and guests from the United States, were E. Stewart, former Superintendent of Forestry for the Dominion; A. H. D. Ross, Lecturer, Faculty of Forestry; Thomas Southworth, Superintendent of Colonization, Toronto; W. C. J. Hall, Superintendent of Forest Protective Service, Quebec; Abraham Knechtel, Inspector of Dominion Forest Reserves, Ottawa; E. J. Zavitz, Forester, Department of Agriculture, Guelph; Ellwood Wilson and Marshall C. Small, Laurentide Paper Co., Grand'Mère; Reginald R. Bradley, Miramichi Paper Co., Chatham, N.B.; G. C. Piche, Department of Lands and Forests, Quebec; and F. W. H. Jacombe, Technical Assistant, Dominion Forest Service, Ottawa (62).

The emphasis on practicability for its own sake seems to have been a constant source of irritation to Dr. Fernow, who argued strongly that one did not expect other professional schools to turn out fully qualified practitioners on graduation, that in all cases the graduate required some experience under supervision to make the best use of his academic education, but that having had such experience, the university-trained man with his background of scientific knowledge and understanding should be far better qualified to reach the practical solution of a wide range of problems than the man whose knowledge and experience are strictly limited. In arguing along these lines, Fernow more than once quoted G. K. Chesterton:

> There has arisen in our time a most singular fancy—the fancy that when things go very wrong, we need a practical man. It would be far truer to say that when things go very wrong, we need an unpractical man. Certainly, at least, we need a theorist. A practical man means a man accustomed to mere daily practice, to the way things commonly work. When things will not work, you must have the thinker, the man who has some doctrine about why they work at all. It is wrong to fiddle while Rome is burning; but it is quite right to study the theory of hydraulics while Rome is burning. (7)

In retrospect, it appears that the forester has been highly successful in demonstrating the practical utility of his calling, even to the extent sometimes of obscuring in the public mind the scientific implications of his ultimate objectives.

In point of fact, opportunities soon developed for the summer employment of undergraduates, probably as a result of the activities of Dr. Fernow and his staff and the many contacts they were able to establish.

Senior students worked during the first summer of the course (1908) with the Turner Lumber Company, surveying and preparing a map for a portion of the limit in Wilson Township near Loring. This work was commended highly by Mr. D. J. Turner, the president of the company, in a letter to Dr. Fernow (41), and at a later date, after employing forestry students for three successive summers, Mr. Turner in speaking before the Foresters' Club[4] said that the work they had done had been most valuable to his company. In the summer of 1909, there were also jobs available in Rondeau Park and in the State of

[4]See p. 82.

Maine, where forest damage caused by a Canadian railroad was being assessed.

In 1910, all undergraduates were employed for the summer, twelve with the Dominion Forestry Branch, nine with the Canadian Pacific Railroad, two with the Pennsylvania Railroad Company, two in Nova Scotia assisting in the reconnaissance survey of that province, five with the Ontario Government, and one with a lumber company. In 1911, the pattern varied somewhat, twenty being with the Dominion Forestry Branch, sixteen with private companies, and four with the Ontario Government.

Permanent employment first became available through the Dominion Forestry Branch. It was largely as a result of the interest of and action taken by R. H. Campbell, Superintendent of Forestry at Ottawa, that early forestry graduates from Toronto and other universities were not only given jobs but placed in key positions in the Forestry Branch soon after graduation. Thus H. R. MacMillan (Yale, '08) was made Assistant Director a year after graduation, and when he moved to British Columbia in 1912 he was succeeded by T. W. Dwight, '10; D. R. Cameron, '11, was made District Inspector of Forest Reserves in British Columbia the year he graduated, and E. H. Finlayson, '11, Inspector in Alberta the year following graduation.

The part the Dominion Forestry Branch played in the employment of forestry graduates during the first few years of the Faculty's existence is shown by the following figures (*14*):

Year of graduation	Total number of graduates	Number of graduates receiving first employment with Dominion Forestry Branch
1909	1	–
1910	2	2
1911	4	2
1912	9	8
1913	11	9
1914	7	5
1915	7	5

Although not a graduate himself, Mr. Campbell was a strong advocate of professional forestry and did a great deal towards getting it established in this country. It may have been as a result of his early affiliation with the Canadian Forestry Association, of which he was secretary for a number of years, but in any case he made the decision that the Dominion Forestry Branch was to be staffed in its supervisory positions with university-trained foresters. His employment policy also provided the opportunity for an increasing number of undergraduates to gain field experience under a wide variety of conditions.

Some of the graduates who began their forestry careers with the Dominion Government later went to British Columbia, where in 1912 a provincial forest service was organized with a professional forester at its head. When, in 1913, the Canadian Pacific Railway undertook a survey of its forest holdings in that province, the demand for graduate foresters increased rapidly; a number of these came from American forest schools as well as from the universities of Toronto, Laval, and New Brunswick. Peter McEwen, '16, has written an interesting account of his experiences on these surveys for three summers (1913–15) while an undergraduate student at Toronto (38).

By 1914, a definite trend in employment was becoming established. While this was interrupted by the war, it could be stated by 1919 that employment opportunities were increasing in every direction. During the war period, the Dominion Government through the Forestry Branch continued its work in connection with forest reserves and the planting of shelterbelts in western Canada, and also laid plans to inaugurate a programme of forest research, for which, in 1916, one hundred square miles in the Petawawa Military District were set aside as a research centre. At the same time the Commission of Conservation extended its surveys to the west to include Saskatchewan and British Columbia (1918), and was supporting a research programme under the direction of Dr. Howe and in co-operation with provincial governments and certain pulp and paper companies in eastern Canada; later this work was incorporated in the research programme of the Forestry Branch.

The provincial governments, being responsible for the administration of much of the accessible forest land in the country, were making increasing use of graduate foresters, as were the forest industries in the planning and organization of their operations. For the period as a whole, approximately sixty graduates of the School were employed by government and fourteen by industry. Employment with government was mainly in administration, fire protection, and regional surveys, while in industry a start was being made with operational surveys and logging.

From the beginning of this period, the Faculty was faced with certain administrative difficulties resulting in part from the gradual deterioration of the general economic situation, which of course affected the whole country, but perhaps more from factors and situations that are almost inevitably associated with the early development of a new university department and a new profession. In this particular case, perhaps the problems of establishment and adjustment were emphasized by the fact that, in contrast to most other professions in which the members themselves first join in associations or societies to provide training facilities for new recruits, with the universities only gradually taking over this responsibility, forestry training in Canada began at once in the university without the support of an established profession and without a background of experience and tradition.

One of the early problems of the new faculty was that of accommodation. For the first few months, classes were held in the old residence of University College. In the following year, more permanent quarters were obtained in a brick residence at the southeast corner of Grosvenor Street and Queen's Park, to which an addition had been built; for the next eighteen years this building was to be shared with the Department of Botany. Dr. Fernow's office was in a front room on the second floor, through the windows of which he could look out on the well-kept lawns of the park. Classrooms and the library were on the first floor, and a large room on the south side was used by the students as a common room. On November 26, 1908, this building was officially opened for the use of the two departments with a reception, the guests being welcomed by Dr. and Mrs. Fernow and Professor Faull[5] of the Department of Botany and Mrs. Faull.

The first few years saw a steady increase in enrolment, and students were soon overflowing the accommodation, causing the Dean to refer with increasing emphasis, in each successive annual report, to the urgent need for more lecture and laboratory space. That the problem was recognized and an attempt made by the University authorities to deal with it will be seen from the President's report for 1914 (the year of highest enrolment in the Faculty for this period with 51 students), where it is stated (pp. 11–12): "In Forestry the need for space was so urgent that it was resolved to secure temporary relief by converting an old stable into a laboratory, but the financial stress has interfered even with this plan."

[5]Appointed Associate Professor in 1907.

Today it is hard to realize that the old residence on Queen's Park Crescent served as the home, or rather the *pied-à-terre*, of both Forestry and Botany for such a long period of time. To the staff it represented mainly a restriction on development that must be overcome—to the students of those days it was the centre of their university life, and as such had a unique value for them, even to the musty, cobwebby basement, where Bottle, the headless horse of diamond-hitch fame[6] and all the paraphernalia for "stunt nite" were kept. Indeed there was some regret when, in 1917, part of this room was remodelled for the use of the gardener.

Another difficulty that persisted over a long period was the lack of proper facilities for field work. In common with any metropolitan university giving courses in natural resource management, the Toronto forestry staff had some difficulty in locating suitable areas for field instruction. Professor White soon exhausted the possibilities on the campus and in Queen's Park, and thereafter expeditions were taken to Lawrence Park and to the Humber Valley. While this satisfied for the time being the requirements of forest botany, much more was needed in other directions. The University announcement (21) of the establishment of a Faculty of Forestry (1907) stated in part, "It is hoped that the government will place a forest reservation at the disposal of the University as practice ground." Expectations of a permanent field station may have been associated in the minds of the administration with the suggestion made by the Royal Commission (1906) (51) that, having in mind the recent settlement of the boundaries of New Ontario, "at least a million acres [in this region] will be set aside for the University and University College" (64). Not that the Faculty of Forestry required anything of this magnitude, but it was to be more than thirty years before a permanent area of any size would be provided. This is rather surprising in view of the often expressed hope and obvious need that the forestry course include instruction and exercises of a practical nature.

Perhaps the nearest the problem came to being solved during this period was on the occasion of a meeting on conservation held in Convocation Hall in 1910, when the Chairman of the Board of Governors of the University, Dr. B. E. Walker, in urging the Minister of Lands, Forests, and Mines (the Honourable Mr. Cochrane) that "the government should turn over to the University of Toronto a large

[6]See p. 84.

area of timber land" for practical experiment, was told in reply, "it will not be hard to persuade the government to act upon that suggestion—the subject is before them" (8). However, nothing came of it. The reason may in part have been one of personality. Both Aubrey White, the Deputy Minister, and Dr. Fernow were men of strong character and, while they were both aiming at the same general objective, they did so with quite different backgrounds and methods of attack, and at times probably did not altogether see eye to eye.

In any case, no permanent practice ground was available, and as a result field work tended to be peripatetic, the students going each year to a different location as arrangements could be made. This had some advantage in acquainting them with a variety of forest types and conditions, but also had serious disadvantages, particularly in there being no provision for the establishment of demonstration areas and the undertaking of long-term investigations, both of which require continuity and progressive records to be useful.

The first field instruction of forestry students in this country was given at Rondeau Park on Lake Erie and later in the Nipissing District, Algonquin Park, in May 1908. The students were J. H. White, F. M. Mitchell, and T. W. Dwight, and the instructor was A. H. D. Ross. Exercises were undertaken in surveying, tree planting, the writing of forest descriptions, cruising, and timber estimating, using both strip and sample-plot methods; a study was made of the silvicultural features of characteristic hardwood types, and the students had the opportunity to see some log driving and other activities of general interest (61).

In the spring of 1909, the senior and junior classes took their field work on the limits of the Strong Lumber Company on the south shore of Lake Nipissing about thirty-six miles west of Callander. There they made a reconnaissance survey of some 6,000 acres and a more detailed survey of 400 acres, prepared a report describing the quantity, species, and quality of timber present, the best method of extracting it, including the location of logging roads, and made a comparative evaluation of the tract for agricultural and forestry purposes (42). In the following spring (1910), the students were on the limits of the Georgian Bay Lumber Company on Nine Mile Lake just south of Bala with a similar programme of work (23). In 1911, a change was made when for the first time the students visited the Provincial Forest Nursery at St. Williams. Here some observations were made on the remnants of the natural forest in the vicinity, and instruction was given on the work of the nursery; there was opportunity for some practical experience in planting techniques and the use of tools specially designed for this work. A number of these had been brought from Germany, including a planting machine which is believed to have been one of the first tested on this continent. Following this initial visit, plans were made for first-year students to spend the whole summer period on various phases of field work at St. Williams (63); while this extensive programme did not materialize, there has been from the beginning a week of instruction at St. Williams at the end of the spring term for the fourth-year students in connection with their course in silviculture, first under Dr. White, and later under Professor Hosie.

In 1912, to meet the demands of employers that students engaged on forestry work during the summer months should report for duty by May 1, the field work, apart from that to be taken at the forest nursery, was changed from the spring to the fall term. The first such fall camp for third- and fourth-year students was held in 1912 on the limits of the John B. Smith & Sons Lumber Company at Franks Bay, Lake Nipissing. For a time the camp was held every second year, in 1914 on the limits of the Graves, Bigwood Lumber Company, north of Nairn, and in 1916 at Thor Lake.[7] The change of the camp period from spring to fall did not by any means satisfy all employers, as the camp programme began early in September before many of the summer jobs were finished.

In addition to the spring and fall practice camps, the third-year students have from the beginning visited a logging operation each year for the purpose of studying methods and equipment and making reports thereon. For many years these trips were made during the Christmas vacation, the first one being held during this period in 1907–8 on the operations of the Graves, Bigwood Lumber Company and the Booth Lumber Company. At first the whole class went together to one camp. Later, however, as numbers increased, it was necessary for the students to go in groups of two or three, each visiting a different logging operation as arrangements could be made.

From what has been said, it is apparent that the lumber companies provided the facilities for much of the field work undertaken in the first few years of the Faculty's existence. While this was undoubtedly

---

[7]Later (about 1921) the fall camp became an annual affair to be attended by fourth-year students only.

appreciated by both staff and students, it was nevertheless recognized that for much of the practical work there should be available permanently a representative forest area reasonably accessible to the Faculty. At the end of the first five years of moving from one field station to another, Dean Fernow expressed strongly his dissatisfaction with this arrangement. The lack of proper facilities for field work and the difficulties in finding adequate lecture and laboratory space led him to say in his annual report for 1912–13 that "after the first quinquennium of its existence, it cannot be said that the Faculty has reached a permanent form."

Limitations imposed by these conditions were emphasized in successive annual reports, and by 1917 the Dean was strongly recommending a reorganization of the Faculty after the war, the main objectives being more adequate accommodation, increased staff, acquisition of a permanent field station, and the extension of study time so as to make the best possible compromise between theory and practical experience in the field. Conditions did not permit the immediate solution of many of these difficulties, and one may wonder if Dr. Fernow did not at times look back rather quizzically to the point in his career when, in acknowledging his nomination for the position of Dean, he enquired of the University authorities whether in fact this position was to be more than "merely a Chair of Forestry," and went on to say that "unless the means for a really efficient department are actually in sight," he would not wish to undertake the task of building it up "by uncertain steps."

That his plans for reorganization were at least well received by the authorities may be judged from the statement made in his last annual report (1919) that "It would appear that the first or pioneering stage of the Faculty is coming to an end and that the organization on the lines suggested in former reports, contemplating increased staff and a permanent practice camp, must soon be inaugurated."

Despite the difficulties, Fernow could be proud of his Faculty for many things, not the least of which was the record of the graduates and undergraduate students in the armed forces of their country. During the war years 76 per cent of the graduates and 43 per cent of the undergraduates and former students—80 in all—enlisted. Of this total, 49 obtained commissions, and 15 were killed in action. Nine were awarded the Military Cross, 4 the Military Medal, and 7 were mentioned in dispatches. This was indeed a record of service of which to be proud. At the same time, the Dean must have felt some concern, for by 1917, as a result of the demands of war, the total undergraduate enrolment had dropped to 9.

Dr. Fernow retired in 1919. He had been in failing health for some time, but held on until the end of the war. In a newsletter dated November 20, 1917, addressed to the University of Toronto foresters overseas, G. A. Mulloy, '18, referred to the rumour that the Dean would retire immediately after the war, and went on to say, "You men, who have not graduated as yet, will be sorry, if this is true." Indeed, the students were greatly attached to both the Dean and Mrs. Fernow, who took a deep personal interest in them, treating them as members of the family. Often on Sunday evenings a number of the students were invited by the Fernows to their home on Admiral Road, where the Dean, an accomplished musician, would play the piano. Mrs. Fernow formed the "Interrogative Club" for the purpose, as she said, of recalling the lost art of conversation. This was a small group of students from all faculties who met regularly once a month to discuss selected subjects that were introduced on each occasion by the presentation of a paper by one of the members.

Mrs. Fernow also contributed to the more formal work of the Faculty by teaching German to the undergraduates. As the classes were small and performance as well as attendance was marked daily, it was inevitable that a good many students obtained a working knowledge of the German language in this way.

Following his retirement in 1919, Dr. Fernow continued to live in Toronto, carrying on his editorial work and an extensive correspondence with his many friends in North America and elsewhere. The contribution he had made to forestry had been recognized on two occasions during his professional career when he received the honorary degree of Doctor of Laws from the University of Wisconsin in 1896, and from Queen's University in 1903. After his retirement, the University of Toronto conferred on him the degree of Doctor of Laws, *honoris causa*, at Convocation on June 3, 1920. On that occasion, the President of the University, Sir Robert Falconer, in introducing Dr. Fernow, said:

Those who have known this University for the past thirteen years, have recognized Dr. Fernow as one of its distinguished figures. Both in the

United States and in Canada, he was the pathfinder, and still remains the outstanding authority as to the theory and the practice of the forester's profession. His knowledge of the subject is unrivalled, his labour in spreading its principles by pen and speech has been unceasing, and his success as an organizer unqualified. A well-educated gentleman of refined tastes and perfect self-control, Dr. Fernow has won the admiration of his students and his colleagues, and he has our deep sympathy in the impairment of his health, which has been partly caused by his unremitting activity over a long life in extending a profession to which he has most unselfishly devoted himself. This degree will be but a slight expression of the gratitude of the University for his services as first Dean of the Faculty of Forestry. (11)

Perhaps the honour that brought him greatest pleasure, in view of the early history associated with it, was the naming of Fernow Hall at Cornell University on October 5, 1922, in recognition of the contribution he had made to American forestry education. On this occasion, there were many at home and abroad who expressed their appreciation for all he had done for forestry in the United States and Canada. The words of the late Henry S. Graves, at that time Dean of the School of Forestry, Yale University, have particular significance in the present context:

... But it was not only in the public work in forestry that he performed a great service. From the very beginning, he insisted upon high technical standards for the professional forester. Under his direction was established the first high-grade technical forest school of the country. The standards, which he set, have had a very great influence upon forest education and upon technical forestry. His subsequent work at Toronto and his many technical writings have always been a great aid in pointing out the objectives of forestry and in upholding the standards upon which our practice must be based. (2)

Owing to poor health, Dr. Fernow had not been able to attend the ceremonies in his honour at Cornell; he died in the following year on February 6 at the age of seventy-two.

III. Further Developments: The Influence of Industrial Expansion and Government Policy

A Challenge to and an Opportunity for the Profession . . .

FOLLOWING THE RETIREMENT of Dean Fernow in 1919, Dr. Howe became Acting Dean, and his appointment as Dean of the Faculty was confirmed in the following year. Dr. Howe was to hold this position for more than twenty years, a period which may conveniently be divided into two nearly equal parts, each representing quite different conditions in our economy and industrial activity. These conditions and the changes associated with them had a marked influence on many aspects of Canadian life, including the progress made by the young profession of forestry.

In this chapter we are concerned with the decade 1919–29, a period of rapid growth and changing values, sometimes referred to in other contexts as "the roaring twenties." From the forestry viewpoint, it is perhaps best remembered by the considerable development of the pulp and paper industry, based on the natural resources of forest and water, and associated with this the formulation of government policy that had as its declared objective the management of the forest resource on a sustained yield basis.

Also as background to this development in policy was the fact that the war of 1914–18 had emphasized the strategic value of timber and the need for governments to plan for assured supplies in the future. In Ontario, this and other factors[1] resulted first in the reorganization and improvement of fire protection services, soon to be followed by an expanded programme of nursery development and reforestation, and the undertaking of primary reconnaissance surveys in various parts of the Province.

[1] As for example, the Matheson fire of 1916 which resulted in serious loss of life as well as much destruction of timber.

As a result of the rapid expansion of the pulp and paper industry during this period and the consequent increase in the demand for wood, more attention was given to problems associated with the harvesting of forest products and their transportation by land and water: in particular to the methods of logging best suited to eastern Canadian conditions and the training of foresters for qualification in this field. While efficient logging had always been recognized as an integral part of forest management, conditions of access, distance and topography, as well as the expanding markets for forest products all tended to emphasize its relative importance in the development of forestry practice in this country. At the same time the increasing demand on the natural forest underlined the need to provide for future requirements, not only through reservation of forest land and more efficient utilization of timber, but, more important, by ensuring adequate regeneration after cutting.

As some measure of the over-all progress made in forestry over the decade, it may be noted that at the beginning foresters were engaged almost exclusively in protection, surveying, reforestation, and investigation; they were not yet responsible in large numbers for the logging department of operating companies or for the administration of Crown lands under licence. By the end of the period, their position had become much more strongly established in both these areas. In the *Annual Ring* for 1952, W. A. Delahey, '14, has given an interesting account of the pioneering work of early graduates with the pulp and paper industry, their difficulties in gaining recognition, and the undoubted success they attained in a fairly short time in establishing the place of the professional forester in that industry. Names he uses by way of illustration include B. F. Avery (Yale) '14, A. W. Bentley, '21, G. G. Cosens, '23, C. B. Davis (Penn. State) '17, J. D. Gilmour, '11, and R. W. Lyons, '16. By 1927, the demand for foresters was greater than ever before, and Dr. Howe could report that in a number of cases with both government and industrial organizations the scope of the forester's activities and the extent of his responsibilities were increasing rapidly. This was particularly true in the industrial field; in comparison with the first decade of the Faculty's existence, when only 20 per cent of the graduates were employed in industry and 80 per cent were in government service, the second decade showed 45 per cent of the graduates with government, 45 per cent with industry, and 10 per cent in university teaching and other occupations.

The impetus given to various aspects of forestry during this period, whether in protection, logging, or the more theoretical concept (at that time) of maintaining forest soil productivity, helped to delineate the probable lines of future development and hence the areas in which professionally trained men would be most needed; this in turn led to a detailed study of school curricula and suggestions for change, both in subject matter and organization.

As Dr. Howe pointed out in the *Annual News Letter of the Foresters' Club*[2] for 1928, a number of proposals had been made (presumably by Alumni) along these lines, one being that the general four-year undergraduate work be reorganized to provide a common course for all students in the first and second years, while in the third and fourth years provision would be made for specialization, either in the biological subjects basic to silviculture or in engineering and related subjects of importance to logging. It had also been suggested that the practice camp be extended over the entire summer at the end of the second year, or alternatively, that the summer previous to entering the Faculty be spent by the candidates in a camp devoted to surveying, dendrology, and mensuration. The latter arrangement would provide an opportunity for student selection as well as student training.

Throughout this period there was a fairly constant increase in enrolment, interrupted briefly in the mid-twenties, apparently as a result of raising the entrance requirements. This and other developments emphasized once again the need that facilities and accommodation be enlarged and improved along the lines that had been recommended repeatedly by Dr. Fernow.

Soon after his appointment as Dean, Dr. Howe had the opportunity to set forth the needs of the Faculty in a report to the Royal Commission on University Finances (1920) (52). In doing so, Dr. Howe recommended that, in the best interests of forestry education in Ontario, provision should be made as soon as possible for (*a*) a permanent practice camp and experimental forest, (*b*) facilities and staff adequate

[2]A student publication of the Foresters' Club of the Faculty issued annually or biennially under various titles over the period 1924–46 and referred to elsewhere in this book as the *News Letter* of the year issued. See Appendix III for complete list.

to provide a graduate programme at the master's level, (c) a subprofessional course for forest rangers, and (d) a forest products museum.³ In his annual report to the President (1921), Dr. Howe again mentioned these objectives, and went on to say, "We shall expect the fulfilment of these plans within the next few years, for without it we cannot obtain our full measure of usefulness in the forestry education of the Province and the Dominion." There can be little quarrel with these objectives, and it would undoubtedly have been of great advantage if at that time facilities could have been provided on the one hand for the postgraduate training of those wishing to qualify for research positions and on the other the proper instruction of forest rangers so that they could assist more effectively in routine field work. However, the attainment of these and other objectives recommended by Dr. Howe was to be a gradual process over many years.

In 1920, there did appear to be a good possibility that a permanent field station would be provided by the Provincial Government. Nothing came of it, however, and for a time the fall camp continued to move about, in 1921 being held on the Timagami Forest Reserve, and in 1922 and 1923 at Gull Lake. In 1924, at the suggestion of W. A. Delahey, '15, and J. H. McDonald, '22, the camp was moved to Achray in Algonquin Park. This arrangement proved highly successful, and as a result plans were made to continue it on a more or less permanent basis; for the next eleven years (1924–34), Achray was the headquarters for fourth-year field training, the work being developed there mainly under the direction of Professor Millar in the first instance, and later Professor Dwight. At the same time other field activities were continued, including the winter logging trip and a week's visit at the St. Williams forest nursery in the spring to study nursery techniques and plantation management.

---

³The Royal Ontario Museum, which was established about this time, made no provision for exhibits relating to the forests and forest industries of the Province. In his annual report for 1920, Dean Howe made the following statement: "The importance of the forests and forest products in the economic life of the Province is practically without representation to the public in the form of museum exhibits. Such exhibits give much space to the economic minerals, yet the forests have contributed four times more revenue to the provincial treasury since Confederation than have the mines. There probably has never been a time when an adequate exhibition of Ontario's forest products would have greater educational power than at present."

In his report to the Royal Commission on University Finances, Dr. Howe made no mention of the most urgent need of the Faculty—a new building—probably because the University authorities were fully aware of the situation. Indeed, in his annual report for 1920-1, the President of the University stated (pp. 8-9): ". . . but inadequate as this Faculty [Forestry] was housed before the war, it is more so now, and, along with Botany, has the worst accommodation of any scientific department in the University." However, as time passed without any action being taken, the Dean, in his report for 1923, stated categorically that the most pressing need of the Faculty was "a new building with more convenient and modern facilities to enable the teaching staff to give the students better instruction."

This proved to be the turning point. In the following year, authority was given to prepare the necessary plans, and in 1925 the new building was completed. The dedication ceremony was held in January 1926, conjointly with annual meetings of the Canadian Forestry Association and the Canadian Society of Forest Engineers. This proved to be one of the largest gatherings of foresters to take place in North America up to that time, with many American and Canadian visitors being present, including more than half of the graduates of the Faculty. It was undoubtedly true, as was stated at the time, that the new building and all that it afforded "put new life into the Faculty, giving an impetus to the work of staff and students alike." It did certainly meet the immediate requirements of the Faculty for undergraduate work, but had little provision for further expansion in this area or for the postgraduate and research programmes that were being planned.

In the meantime, the staff had been considerably strengthened with the return of Professor Millar from military service at the beginning of 1919, and the appointment of T. W. Dwight as Associate Professor in 1923 and R. C. Hosie as Teaching Assistant in 1924. Mr. Dwight, who graduated from the Faculty in 1910, and qualified for his master's degree at Yale the following year, was Assistant Director of the Dominion Forest Service at the time of his appointment; Mr. Hosie had just completed his undergraduate course in forestry in 1924, having entered the University soon after his demobilization from the Canadian Army, in which he served overseas with the Fourth Canadian Mounted Rifles. For most of this period then, the Faculty had a staff of five full-time members, including Dean Howe and Dr. White, who was promoted to the rank of full professor in 1927.

Much of the time of staff members was devoted to extra-curricular activities, some within the forestry programme of the Provincial Government, while others were aimed at increasing the knowledge of the general public on forestry affairs. Earlier, Dr. Fernow had emphasized the responsibility of the Faculty in giving leadership in public education, and to this end had addressed innumerable audiences and written many articles for publication in the popular press. Dean Howe continued these activities with the object of gaining increased interest and support for forestry, his view, as he expressed it, being that "our forests will never be adequately protected from fire and managed on a basis of periodic cropping until the majority of the people demand these things." An indefatigable conservationist and a writer of some distinction, Dean Howe contributed articles or editorial comment to nearly every issue of *Forest and Outdoors* during this decade; he also contributed in many other ways to the activities of the Canadian Forestry Association, being a director for a number of years and serving as president during 1923.

To assist in one aspect of public education, that of acquainting the layman with the trees growing in Ontario and providing the student with a reliable reference work for identification, Professor White in 1925 completed a bulletin, *The Forest Trees of Ontario and the more commonly planted foreign trees*, which was published by the Department of Lands and Forests. This book, which has been used widely by government and educational institutions, was revised by Professor Hosie in 1946.

Professor White continued to work closely with the Ontario Forestry Branch on a part-time basis after 1919, as by then he had resumed his lectures in the Faculty. Following the reorganization of the fire protection service, in which he played an important part, he was involved in the planning and supervising of extensive reconnaissance and inventory surveys that were to provide information on which to base plans for the administration of the provincial forests. As a result of these surveys made in 1920, 1921, and 1922, and the recommendations of those in charge of them, including A. B. Connell, '14, R. N. Johnston, '17, Gordon Dallyn, '16, Peter McEwen, '16, and

Wallace Delahey, '15, the first three forest districts in Ontario were created with headquarters at Parry Sound, Pembroke, and Tweed. In February 1922, Dallyn was appointed district forester in Tweed, Delahey in Pembroke, and McEwen in Parry Sound.

To assist directly with the problem of fire protection and to promote further the idea of a forest ranger school, a short course of lectures was given in 1928-9 by the Faculty and staff of the Department to the chief rangers and deputy chief rangers of the provincial Forest Protection service.

Perhaps 1927 (just twenty years after the Faculty was established) can be looked upon as the most significant year for forestry in Ontario during this period, both in retrospect and prospect. In his report for 1926-7, Dr. Howe noted a marked improvement during the previous ten years in the attitudes of government, private industry, and the general public towards the work of graduate foresters, who were increasingly taking over the responsibility of organizing and administering all the technical matters pertaining to the management of the forest resource.

About this time, the Ontario Government initiated a definite forest management policy, and stated publicly that it was seeking the cooperation of the Faculty in carrying it out. To implement this policy in part, the Forestry Act[4] was passed (1926), giving the Government power to create forest reserves from townships unfit for agricultural development; also in keeping with the provisions of this Act, the Lieutenant-Governor-in-Council established on June 21, 1927, a Forestry Board, and appointed to the membership thereof J. A. Gillies, Braeside, B. F. Avery, Sault Ste. Marie, H. G. Schanche, Iroquois Falls, E. J. Zavitz (Deputy Minister of Forestry), Toronto, and Dr. C. D. Howe, Toronto. It was stated in the proclamation and Order-in-Council relating to this Board that its purpose was to carry on "research work in connection with the forest lands of the Province of Ontario and to study all questions in connection with the planting, growth, development, marketing, and reproduction of pulpwoods on the Crown lands and on the lands of Crown lessees, licensees, and concessionaires in the Province of Ontario" (49).

Progress with forest policy and legislation in Ontario over this

[4]17 Geo. V, c. 41, s. 1 (Ont.).

decade culminated in the passing in 1929 of the Pulpwood Conservation Act[5] and the Provincial Forests Act.[6] The significance of these events was commented on by Dr. Howe in the *News Letter* of that year as follows:

From a forestry standpoint, the third session of the 17th legislature of Ontario will go down in history as the beginning of a new epoch. It will mark the time that the terms "sustained yield," "the balancing of consumption and production," and "the best forestry practice," were first written into forestry legislation in Ontario . . . . Above all, the legislation of 1929 will be epoch-making, because it will mark the inauguration of an attempt to place the pulp and paper industry of the Province "on a permanent basis with respect to raw material, so that the industry may have an assured source of supply" to quote one of the acts; also, because it will mark the placing of approximately 20,000 square miles of forests under the control of foresters in order "gradually to bring them under a sustained-yield basis" to quote from the other act.

He concluded that "the recent legislation is a challenge to and an opportunity for the profession such as it never had before in this Province."

It was indeed a challenge, though one that would require a great deal more knowledge, both technical and economic, before it could be met successfully. Professor White, writing in the same *News Letter* (1929) on developments in forestry practice over the years, after pointing out that for the first decade these had been mainly in administration and protection, and for the second decade they had extended into logging operations, went on to say, "Foresters are faced with their next task—that of establishing the technical basis of forest management. It means much research and experiment, and only a beginning has as yet been made. . . . This situation will call for still more intensive training in forestry and will create opportunity for the man who is specially trained for investigative work or who is strongly grounded in the fields basic to management."

Certainly progress in forestry could not depend solely on changes in policy and the passing of legislation, but required far more knowledge of the forest itself. While surveys had been carried out and research started during the previous decade, mainly by the Commission of Conservation and more recently through the activities of the

[5]19 Geo. V, c. 13 (Ont.).
[6]19 Geo. V, c. 14 (Ont.).

First field instruction to be given forestry students in Canada—Rondeau Park, 1908. *From left to right*: J. H. White, B. E. Fernow, A. H. D. Ross, T. W. Dwight, F. M. Mitchell

Second Annual Forestry Dinner held at McConkey's Restaurant on January 30, 1913. BACK ROW (*left to right*): A. H. D. Ross, R. D. Prettie, *unidentified*, E. J. Zavitz, D. R. Cameron, R. H. Campbell, Sir Robert Falconer, G. M. Dallyn, H. R. Christie, Dr. B. E. Fernow, H. A. Parker, E. Wilson, C. Leavitt, C. D. Howe, W. N. Millar, W. Boyd, J. Alexander, A. M. Thurston, G. S. Smith, W. M. Pearce, E. S. Davison, P. Robinson. THIRD ROW: G. Tunstell, F. B. Robertson, J. H. White, J. M. Sloan, C. R. Mills, E. H. Finlayson, W. Kynoch, A. K. Shives, F. S. Newman, F. McVickar, D. Greig, R. M. Watt, G. E. Bothwell, R. L. Campbell, E. B. Prowd, *unidentified*, J. Kay (?), *unidentified*. SECOND ROW: A. E. Parlow, J. L. Simmons, A. B. Connell, S. H. Clark, G. W. Bayly, D. E. Clark, T. F. Rance, C. H. Morse, H. M. Hughson (?), E. C. Manning. FRONT ROW: W. A. Delahey, J. F. L. Hughes, D. German, A. W. Bentley

Gathering of students and Alumni with visitors from the United States and members of the Canadian Society of Forest Engineers and the Canadian Forestry Association on the occasion of the dedication of the Forestry Building, January 21, 1926. FRONT ROW (*left to right*): G. R. Lane, unidentified, S. N. Cooper, B. Claridge, G. W. Phipps, H. P. Webb, W. N. Millar, C. H. Mors, A. H. Richardson, E. Wilson, S. T. Dana, C. D. Howe, C. Leavitt, J. H. White, B. F. Avery, E. H. Finlayson, R. D. Craig, F. S. Newman, B. M. Winegar, J. A. Wilson, C. R. Mills, W. A. Delahey, G. M. Dallyn, C. E. Westland. SECOND ROW: W. C. Lowdermilk, K. G. Fensom, J. Johnston, G. H. Bayly, J. F. Turnbull, W. A. E. Pepler, unidentified, W. M. Robertson, R. H. Candy, N. M. Ross, H. Edgecombe, G. M. Linton, J. L. Simmons, W. H. Haddow, T. W. Dwight, D. R. Cameron, E. McDougall, V. Beede, A. R. Mackenzie, H. H. Parsons, M. Ardenne, I. C. Marritt, W. B. Greenwood, T. E. Mackey, T. H. Ryan, H. H. Krug, J. A. Brodie, L. R. Seheult, C. E. Foote, F. Hatch, E. Hipwell, N. A. Armstrong. THIRD ROW: G. G. Cosens, H. W. Crosbie, J. A. MacDonald, J. L. Van Camp, J. V. Stewart, K. Stewart, J. F. Sharpe, W. Kilby, E. J. Zavitz, H. I. Stevenson, A. F. V. Atkinson, A. H. Burk, R. A. N. Johnston, F. T. Jenkins, W. D. Cram, N. M. Kensit, W. E. McCraw, M. M. Putnam, R. L. Campbell, M. A. Adamson, J. A. Teasdale, J. H. McDonald, D. W. R. Day. FOURTH ROW: W. E. Steele, P. Addison, H. W. McCausland, R. F. Goodall

At a special convocation on the occasion of the Fiftieth Anniversary of the Faculty of Forestry, the University conferred the degree of Doctor of Laws *honoris causa* on Avila Bedard, W. A. Delahey, J. Miles Gibson, R. W. Lyons, H. R. MacMillan, and E. J. Zavitz.

Members of Staff and Alumni, Faculty of Forestry 1960. Front row (*left to right*): W. A. Delahey, E. J. Zavitz, G. G. Cosens, J. W. B. Sisam, T. W. Dwight, R. C. Hosie. Second row: Miss M. H. Harman, Mrs. W. J. McJannet, Miss P. M. Balme. Third row: F. M. Buckingham, J. L. Farrar, N. L. Kissick, E. Jorgensen, A. S. Michell, K. A. Armson, A. D. Hall, D. V. Love

Faculty of Forestry football team 1950—winners of the intramural football championship and Mulock Cup. FRONT ROW (*left to right*): B. F. Merwin, J. A. G. Waddell, M. B. Price, D. T. Bell, T. R. White, R. J. Burgar, G. R. Whitcombe (Captain), H. H. H. Devries, V. J. J. Magnus, W. K. Clark. SECOND ROW: R. W. Booth, D. L. Cunningham, R. W. Morison, A. E. Davis, J. P. McKay, S. B. Sheldon, P. G. Masterson, F. T. Collict, W. C. Dowsett. BACK ROW: J. H. Hewetson, W. W. Hall, Max Lister (Coach), J. W. Keenan, Dean Sisam, A. D. Hundt, E. Markus, D. E. Honeyborne, W. C. Seeley, W. E. Beatty, R. W. Nelson, P. R. Austin, B. R. Duff.

Faculty of Forestry basketball team 1930—winners of the intramural basketball championship and Sifton Cup. FRONT ROW (*left to right*): J. B. Millar (Manager), W. D. Start, E. E. Grainger (Captain), F. N. Wiley, J. Raeburn. BACK ROW: J. Townson, L. E. Simpson, F. Leslie, D. W. Gray.

Left: Number 11 Queen's Park where the accommodation was shared by the Faculty of Forestry and the Department of Botany for 17 years—1908–25. Right: The Forestry Building, which was completed in 1925 and moved to a new location in 1958, as it appeared in 1960

The Ontario Forest Ranger School situated in the centre of the University Forest near Dorset, Ontario

Glendon Hall Botany and Forestry Laboratories and Greenhouse, just completed November 1960

Wood Technology Laboratory added to the Forestry Building at the time it was moved in 1958

Dominion Forest Service[7] (13), little had actually been done to study the problems affecting the forest management in Ontario. As pointed out in an editorial in *Forest and Outdoors* for April, 1929 (with reference to the situation in Ontario), "The necessary legislation is there. All that now remains is action—intelligent action—the only key for which is research."

The Forestry Board had been appointed to plan, organize, and direct investigations along these lines, and three members of the Faculty staff, Professors White, Dwight, and Hosie undertook work on the following projects under the general supervision of the Board and in co-operation with the staff of the Ontario Forestry Branch:

(i) a study of the growth and yield of pulpwood stands in northern Ontario,

(ii) the classification of forest types of Ontario,

(iii) a study of the effect of slash burning on the regeneration of pulpwood species,

(iv) a study of the economic and forest conditions of certain areas in central Ontario with the object of determining their suitability for reservation.

In 1929, Professor White was appointed chairman of a forestry research committee under the Board, to be responsible for the organization of a research programme, with the Wanapetei Forest being set aside as the centre for this work in northern Ontario. This programme was continued until 1932, when, owing to the economic depression, it was not possible to obtain the money necessary for its support.

The 1920's represented a period of tremendous activity in many fields. In forestry, much, though not all, of the activity was constructive and progressive. During this period the function and responsibility of the graduate forester became clearer, and a definite demand for his services developed both in industry and government. These developments were associated in part with economic expansion and in part with a related progressive change in government policy. The rapid growth of the pulp and paper industry resulted in the opening up of new forest areas, the carrying out of surveys to determine the wood capital available, and some improvement in the methods and equip-

[7]When the Commission of Conservation was abolished in 1921, much of its work was taken over by the Dominion Forest Service.

ment for harvesting the mature timber. As the demand for forest products increased, it was soon realized that not only was it important to protect the existing forest from destruction, but also to ensure the continuance of the productivity of forest land; and that progress in these matters would require the solution of many associated economic and technical problems.

At the conclusion of this decade, Dr. Howe stated in his annual report (1929) that there was an increasing interest in forestry matters by the people of the Province, that a number of research projects were under way, and that the Faculty had the largest total enrolment of students since its establishment. He could have added that a beginning had been made with postgraduate studies, as the first two master's degrees in forestry were awarded in 1927 and 1929.

Unfortunately, there was not going to be sufficient time for the forestry plans and programmes of 1929 to develop fully in a favourable economic climate; much of the apparent progress was ephemeral and not sufficiently well rooted in knowledge and experience to withstand the hazards that lay ahead.

IV. Forestry Under Low Pressure 1929-39

The present state of affairs has brought up new and very critical problems. . . .

THE GREAT DEPRESSION, which began towards the end of 1929 and continued through much of the thirties, affected all aspects of Canada's economy as it did that of most countries; it provided an environment for planning and development quite different from that of the previous decade.

In forestry its effects were important and varied, depending in part on local situations and problems, in part on the extent to which forestry principles and practices had become established from one place to another, and also perhaps on the knowledge and perspective of those in authority.

One immediate effect was a curtailment in the demand for wood products, which in turn indicated the highly competitive nature of the forest industries and emphasized further the need for maximum efficiency and low costs in the harvesting and transportation of wood. J. D. Gilmour, '11, had this in mind when, in an article written for the *News Letter* of 1934, he urged the students of the Faculty to aim at being "consummate loggers," and pointed out that "the most efficient logging management is going to be called for in order to meet the conditions of keen competition . . ."

Also, as a reaction to restricted markets and the development of new synthetic materials, efforts were made to give greater emphasis to wood as an industrial material and to develop means for improving its usefulness and marketability.

At the same time, in the minds of some people, the difficulties of the period tended to depreciate the importance of timber production as a primary objective of forestry in a country with extensive natural forests. Perhaps partly as a result of this, but more directly associated with the serious drought conditions and floods that occurred in different parts of North America, increasing interest and attention was given to the protection values of forest cover. In the United States, this period saw the promotion of a number of forestry and other conservation programmes, partly to provide employment, partly to promote integrated regional development, and partly to protect and stabilize soil and water resources.

Another phase of forest use that received increasing attention was that associated with outdoor recreation and wild-life management. In this connection, it is of interest that in Ontario in 1930 Algonquin Park was placed in charge of a professional forester (F. A. MacDougall, '23) after 37 years of ranger staff supervision. From his own experience as Superintendent of the Park, Mr. MacDougall discussed in the *News Letter* of 1934 the opportunities of the forester in game and recreational management, both as investigator and administrator, and additional training the forester might require to qualify for this work.

For the Faculty, the most immediate and serious effect of the depression was the curtailment of forestry work and the consequent reduction of employment opportunities for graduates and undergraduates. In Ontario, at least, the effects of the depression on professional employment were markedly different, both in direction and timing, in the forest industries and government.

During the period 1925–9, the pulp and paper industry had employed about half the graduates of the Faculty in permanent positions and provided about the same proportion of undergraduates with summer work. With the onset of the depression retrenchment began, affecting employment in all phases of the industry including forestry. By 1930, there were no jobs for graduates in this industry, and in a number of cases existing staff was being reduced. However, there was a slight improvement during the following year, and in the course of the next few years a gradual redevelopment of the industry took place and with it the employment of more graduates; this was influenced in part by the recognition that in a number of cases logging operations in charge of foresters were providing relatively low cost wood at the mill (*31*).

In contrast with industry, government departments did not curtail their forestry programmes immediately at the onset of the depression, as in many cases they were involved with essential protection services and research programmes that could not be terminated immediately without considerable waste.

This was true of the Ontario Government, which also was interested in implementing its recent legislation,[1] and in 1930 was expanding its staff with this in mind. Thus, of the eleven men graduating from the Faculty in that year, nine went with the Department of Lands and Forests, one to British Columbia, and one to the Dominion Forest Service. At this time Ontario had the largest staff of professionally trained foresters of any organization in Canada, and Dean Howe in his annual report (1930) made the comment, "This speaks for itself in regard to the enlightened and progressive policy of the Provincial Government in the matter of developing and conserving its forest resources." The situation and the view of Dr. Howe were both to change drastically in the next few years.

By 1932, as the depression continued and many government forestry activities at both provincial and federal levels were brought to a halt, the situation was described by Dean Howe in his annual report for that year as follows:

Owing to the continuance of the business depression, forestry activities throughout the Dominion are practically at a standstill, contraction has taken place in both governmental and private organizations, and many foresters are without employment. Appropriations for stock-taking surveys, reforestation, and research have been greatly curtailed or completely suspended. About the only effort consists in keeping alive the forest protection services, but even these have suffered curtailment. The latter is a very poor form of economy, as the results during the fire hazard season will undoubtedly prove.

A further analysis of the situation was made by the Dean in the *News Letter* for 1933 as follows:

Looking back twenty-five years, we can see a great deal of progress. The present state of affairs, however, has brought up new and very critical problems which require more thoughtful consideration, more concentrated and co-operative effort than we have been called upon to exert in the past ... the public should be led to such an appreciation of the importance of our objectives in terms of intelligent and orderly development of land use and of the forest industries, that it would not endure without protest the abandonment or serious curtailment of great reforestation projects, the reduction of fire protection services to a dangerous limit, and the wiping out of practically all investigative work upon which any sensible policy of handling our forest resources must be based.

[1] The Pulpwood Conservation Act and the Provincial Forests Act.

Indeed, by 1932 forest research activities in Ontario had been greatly curtailed; in papers prepared about this time (31, 32) Dean Howe argued strongly for much greater support in this area, his view being that only through knowledge gained by careful scientific research, with reference for example to the silvicultural characteristics of commercial tree species, could the forest management policy of the government be implemented when economic conditions became more favourable. In this connection, he urged all practising foresters to look upon research as "the keynote to their profession" and support it accordingly. He also emphasized the need for having forestry research properly organized, citing as examples of what he had in mind the National Research Council and the Ontario Research Foundation. One result of his efforts, and that of others similarly aware of the problem, was the establishment in 1933 of an Associate Committee on Forestry by the National Research Council.

During the following years the situation in Ontario continued to deteriorate, and by 1936 the government appeared to have lost all interest in its forestry programme. In that year, the decision was made to stop all forest investigative work and to replace professional with non-professional staff for much of the administrative and protection work of the Department of Lands and Forests. Not only did this bring to an end the employment of new graduates, but resulted in the release of twenty professional foresters from the staff. In retrospect, this action of the Ontario Government can be viewed only as a backward step taken mistakenly in the name of economy, and this at a time when the country was just beginning to recover from the depression. Furthermore, it indicated that beyond a certain point the forestry profession had not been successful in presenting its case to the general public or to their political representatives.

In the industrial field by 1936, there was a definite improvement in employment opportunities, twelve of the fourteen graduates for that year obtaining work in the pulp and paper industry immediately on graduation. This situation continued in the following years with the exception of 1938, when there was a further temporary recession in business activity.

Also in 1936, a co-operative scheme, to be known as the "National Forestry Program" was inaugurated by the Dominion Forest Service for the purpose of assisting the unemployed youth of the country. Many professionally trained men, including foresters, were employed in a supervisory capacity in connection with this programme in 1937, 1938, and 1939.

At the beginning of this period the enrolment in the Faculty was as high as it had ever been, and despite the subsequent difficulties of obtaining employment, there were few withdrawals. However, as the depression continued during the early 1930's there was a rapid decline in first-year registration, that of 1933 being half the number of the previous year. The trend reversed itself a little later, as economic conditions improved, and by 1939 first-year enrolment was very nearly at the same level as in the late 1920's.

As a by-product of the economic situation and in an effort to qualify graduates more fully for employment with forest industry, the Faculty in 1932 began a revision of the curriculum. As noted elsewhere (see chapter VI), a questionnaire was sent out to members of the Alumni, and following an evaluation of the returns, a number of subjects were added to the undergraduate course.

With regard to the staff, Professor Millar, who had been with the Faculty since 1914 except for a short period during the First World War, resigned in 1932, and died in the following year while engaged in work as superintendent of the Civilian Conservation Corps camp at Martinsville, Indiana. It was not possible to name his successor immediately, and during the session 1932–3 a series of special lectures in forest protection and utilization were given by B. F. Avery, at that time with the Abitibi Power & Paper Company Limited, J. D. Gilmour of the Anglo-Canadian Pulp and Paper Company, and H. E. Kedey, K. A. Stewart, and J. F. Sharpe of the Ontario Forestry Branch. These lectures were highly successful, so much so, that it was intended to continue them in the following year. This became unnecessary, however, with the appointment of Gordon G. Cosens as Associate Professor. Mr. Cosens had taken his undergraduate degree in 1923, and was the first graduate student to complete the requirements in forestry for a master's degree at the University of Toronto; he received his M.A. in 1927. During his undergraduate years and for five years after graduation, he worked with the Laurentide Company in Quebec. In 1928 he joined the Spruce Falls Power and Paper Company, Limited, at Kapuskasing as Chief Forester and Assistant Manager of Woodlands, resigning from that company in 1934 to join the Faculty.

During the early part of the period under discussion, the fall camp had continued at Achray with only the fourth-year students receiving field instruction there; this arrangement was criticized by Alumni engaged in industrial forestry, their view being that the students did not have sufficient opportunity for practical field work under supervision.

Dean Howe and other members of the Faculty staff continued to press for a permanent practice area reasonably accessible to Toronto where continuity of work would be possible and long-term management plans developed. By 1936, the first important step towards this objective was taken by moving the location of the field camp from Achray. In commenting on this proposed move in his report for 1936, Dr. Howe said:

Since it is probable that most of our men will go to private industries for the next few years at least, we have arranged our practice camp so as to give the students a more intensive training in woods work. Instead of six weeks at the beginning of fourth year, the practice camp work hereafter will be given for three weeks at the end of the first, second, and third years. The site of the camp has been transferred from Algonquin Park to a more accessible area in Haliburton County. It also has a greater variety of forest conditions. The area is being carefully studied and surveyed from the standpoint of a permanent location.

The subsequent steps taken to establish a permanent field station and ranger school—thus attaining two of the objectives set out in Dr. Howe's brief to the Royal Commission of 1920 (52)—are discussed in some detail in chapter VIII.

In looking back on this period, it may be said for forestry, as no doubt for many other areas of human activity, that while the promises of the previous decade were not fulfilled, there was the opportunity and indeed the necessity to review and reassess aims and methods, both in practice and in training. In the end, this probably had some value in laying a stronger foundation for the future. In the meantime, however, it could mean considerable loss to the profession and the Province, both in trained personnel and in technical development; as it turned out, conditions favourable to further progress in forestry in Ontario and elsewhere in Canada were soon in evidence.

V. War and Post-War 1939-60

There is nothing that needs to be more strongly emphasized and impressed upon the young professional forester than that . . . his main obligation is the replacement of the crop he has harvested, whether produced by unaided nature or otherwise, by as good if not better crop of timber than he found (B. E. FERNOW).

THIS RELATIVELY LONG period, although interspersed by wars and rumours of war and showing considerable evidence of unrest and instability in many areas, was characterized in North America generally by industrial growth and an expanding economy. The demand for forest products and services increased rapidly and associated with this the forestry programmes that had been interrupted earlier were resumed and expanded in preparation for what would probably be even greater future demands. In Ontario, having in mind the statutory policy of sustained yield management, special attention was given to problems affecting the maintenance of forest soil productivity through regeneration.

By 1939 there was a definite improvement in the general economic situation, and soon in response to the demands of war there was a further and rapid expansion of both primary and secondary industries. Once again, as had happened in other places and at other times, the value of wood as a strategic material was soon recognized, and supplies were placed under strict government control. This situation and other factors once again brought to the fore the importance of the protection and management of the forest resource in order to ensure adequate supplies of timber for the future.

In this connection, it is interesting to recall the discussions and investigations that took place during the war period, and indeed as a reaction to war-time conditions, by government-sponsored groups and various organizations seeking a basis for the post-war reconstruction of Canada's economy and the rehabilitation of its people who were serving in the armed forces. Much of this study and planning was concerned with a better approach to the management of Canada's natural resources, including her forests. Two undertakings along these lines that may be mentioned are, first, an investigation made by the Advisory Committee on Reconstruction appointed by the federal government in 1943, the report of which includes a number of important recommendations on forestry (1), and second, a series of papers delivered at the University of Toronto in 1943 (3) on various subjects, including the forest resource, considered significant in any programme of economic reconstruction.

The period following the Second World War has been one of growth and expansion unparalleled in our earlier history. While the plans and recommendations made during the war undoubtedly had important results, the main factors responsible for post-war development appear to have been a rapid increase in population, discovery of new mineral wealth, the expansion of our manufacturing in contrast to primary industries, and the continued demand for our exports in foreign markets. The pulp and paper industry has made an outstanding contribution to the country's economy during this period.

Running parallel with our economic expansion has been an increasing concern by those in authority about its nature and the steps that should be taken to ensure its continuance. Conferences have been held to investigate and report on these matters. Surveys of various kinds and for various purposes have been carried out by government and private enterprise, and Royal and other commissions have been appointed by the federal and provincial governments to study many problems, including how best to manage our natural, renewable resources. In Ontario, a Royal Commission on Forestry submitted its report (50) to the Provincial Government in 1947. On the basis of its study, a number of recommendations were made, mainly of an operational and administrative nature; among these was the setting up of an advisory committee to the Minister of Lands and Forests on which education was to be represented. Such a committee was established under Order-in-Council in December 1950, and has continued to function during the intervening period with the Dean of the Faculty of Forestry acting as chairman throughout.

As has been pointed out in earlier chapters, members of the Faculty repeatedly urged that more emphasis on forestry research was a matter of paramount importance and associated with this the provision of staff and facilities for postgraduate training at the universities. There has undoubtedly been some progress along these lines over the past fifteen years, due, in part at least, to changes in the viewpoints of both government and industry towards research generally and also to the gradual recognition by those in authority of its importance in the field of forestry.

Among the factors influencing the general trend have been the demands of war itself, the implications of atomic power, the urge towards improved health and higher standards of living, all of which have given a tremendous impetus to research. In addition, the reports and recommendations of the many committees set up to study conditions affecting our economic well-being have indicated many of the forestry problems requiring investigation. Moreover, there has been the urgent need to deal with specific problems such as the outbreaks of the spruce sawfly, the spruce budworm, and the widespread incidence of the birch dieback; this also has had a direct bearing on developments in forestry research in recent years. And in Ontario, first the Ontario Research Council and later the Ontario Research Foundation have given valuable support to forestry research undertaken by various authorities, including the University.

Thus it has been in an environment of economic expansion and concern for the future that forestry practice and forestry education have been shaped during the past fifteen years.

By 1939 the demand for graduate foresters and hence the opportunity for employment in the profession was definitely improving. In Ontario, this came about in the first instance as a result of industrial activity followed by the Provincial Government resuming the forestry programme that had been brought to a halt during the depression; this trend was supported by the appointment in 1941 of a professional forester, F. A. MacDougall, '23, as Deputy Minister. In 1940, the Department of Lands and Forests employed all the graduates of the Faculty for that year and took a number of undergraduates for summer field work. By 1942, there was a definite shortage of graduate foresters to meet the demand, and this situation continued and became increasingly acute each year during the war and for some time thereafter. The difficulty was due, not only to the resumption of government programmes and the expansion of wood-using industries for war purposes, but also to the relatively small numbers that graduated just prior to the war and the fact that a large number of foresters enlisted in the Armed Services and the Forestry Corps. Furthermore, during the war many undergraduates enlisted before completing their course, so that the number graduating and available for professional work continued at a low level.[1] As recorded in the *News Letter* for 1944, there were at that time 81 graduates, 39 undergraduates, and 22 former students of the Faculty enlisted for overseas service.

By the end of the war, the need for many more trained foresters was urgent. In his report to the President of the University for 1944, Dean Cosens (who had succeeded Dr. Howe in 1941) pointed out that "with approximately one-third of all the graduates in forestry in the armed services and small prospects of additional graduates in the near future, there is a definite shortage of technical foresters. This is handicapping the woodland operations of the lumber and pulp and paper industries and the related government services."

However, at the end of hostilities it soon became apparent that, given a little time, the most urgent immediate requirements for foresters would be met. A relatively large number of ex-service men were interested in making forestry their career, and the total enrolment in the Faculty increased from 45 in 1943–4 to an all-time high of 305 in 1948–9, the latter figure being four times the largest previous enrolment in the Faculty.

Applications for admission were so numerous that some limitation had to be placed on first-year registration, and preference was given to ex-service men, individual selection being based on length of service and academic qualifications; this, of course, greatly curtailed the number of high school students that could be accepted.

Within the Forestry Building itself, some adjustments were made to accommodate these large numbers; two new laboratories were built in the basement and extra seating provided in laboratory and lecture rooms. This and the repetition of lecture and laboratory periods made it possible to provide the regular course for all students.

Within the five-year period 1948–52, the Faculty graduated nearly as many foresters as during the preceding forty years—314 compared with 339. Partly because of the deficiency in technical manpower

---

[1]A total of 28 graduated during the five-year period 1941–5.

that had developed during the war, and partly because of the expanding economy of the post-war years, a high percentage, at least 95 per cent, of these graduates obtained permanent positions in their profession, the majority in Ontario, some in other provinces, and a few outside Canada.

By 1952, the immediate demand was satisfied, and for the next few years employment opportunities declined, with the result that first-year enrolment dropped off, reaching a low of ten entering the Faculty in 1955. Since then, there has been a gradual but steady improvement in employment and a comparable increase in enrolment for both undergraduate and postgraduate work.

During the period under review, there have been a number of changes in and additions to the Faculty staff as the first generation of teachers completed its span.

In 1941, Dr. Howe, who had joined the staff the year after the Faculty was established in 1908, retired and, as we have seen, was succeeded by Professor Cosens. While Dean of the Faculty, Dr. Howe had taken a leading part in many aspects of forestry work. He was one of the early pioneers in forestry research in this country, first in his work with the Commission of Conservation and later with the Ontario Department of Lands and Forests. But he was perhaps best known as a teacher, not only in the education of professional foresters, but also in his constant efforts to promote a wider knowledge and understanding of forestry objectives among the general public. Dr. Howe also played a leading part in the various organizations concerned with the development of forestry in this country; he was President of the Canadian Forestry Association in 1923 and a member of its board of directors for a number of years; he was President of the Canadian Society of Forest Engineers for three years (1924–6), Chairman of the Advisory Board, Department of Lands and Forests, from 1928 to 1932, and a member of the Associate Committee on Forestry for the National Research Council from 1933 to 1939.

In recognition of the contribution he had made to Canadian forestry and forestry education, the University of Toronto conferred on him the degree of Doctor of Laws, *honoris causa*, at Convocation in May, 1943. Following a brief illness in February 1946, Dr. Howe died at the age of seventy-one years.

Just prior to his retirement, Dr. Howe had reiterated an earlier recommendation that the University should establish an introductory course on Canada's natural resources and their management, to be given in the first place to students in certain of the professional faculties and the Faculty of Arts. He based this recommendation on the fact that the natural resources, including soil, mines, waterpower, fish, game, and forests, provide much of the foundation for the material prosperity of the country, and it would seem only reasonable that its potential leaders should have a better understanding of the conditions and problems involved in their management. This proposal was not adopted, and indeed was subject to considerable opposition in the University, due perhaps to a misunderstanding of its purpose and proposed method of presentation.

In 1946, Dr. J. H. White retired after thirty-five years of service with the Faculty, during which he established himself as one of the outstanding teachers in forestry on this continent. Through the action of the Board of Governors, Dr. White was appointed Professor Emeritus in Forestry. Also in recognition of the contribution he had made to forestry and forestry education in Ontario, a number of his former students arranged for a forest area within the St. Williams Nursery Station to be named in his honour the "J. H. White Forest." Dr. White died at his home in Toronto in 1957 at the age of eighty-two.

To provide replacements and help meet the problems of increased enrolment at the end of the war, it was necessary to add new members to the staff. In 1945 J. W. B. Sisam[2] was appointed Associate Professor with teaching responsibilities mainly in Wood Technology and Forest Botany, and in the following year, D. V. Love[3] and A. S. Michell[4] were appointed Assistant Professors, the former to be respon-

[2]J. W. B. Sisam, a graduate of the University of New Brunswick (1931), took his master's degree at Yale in 1937; he was engaged in silvicultural research with the Dominion Forest Service from 1931 to 1939, when he was appointed first Deputy Director and later Director of the Commonwealth Forestry Bureau, Oxford. He received the degree of Doctor of Science, *honoris causa*, from the University of New Brunswick in 1956.

[3]D. V. Love, a graduate of the University of New Brunswick (1941), served with the Royal Canadian Navy from 1942 to 1945. In 1946 he took his master's degree at the University of Michigan, and was employed with Marathon Paper Mills of Canada at the time of his appointment to the Faculty. Professor Love became Associate Professor in 1953, and has acted as Secretary of the Faculty from 1950 to the present time.

[4]A. S. Michell graduated from the Faculty in 1940, and after some field experience with both the government service and industry enlisted in the Royal Canadian

WAR AND POST-WAR 1939-60 55

sible for Forest Economics and certain aspects of Forest Mensuration, and the latter for Logging and Wood Utilization. Also during this period, F. G. Jackson, '31, and J. A. C. Grant, '47, were on the Faculty staff as Instructors, the former for the period 1946 to 1952, and the latter from 1947 to 1952.

In 1947, Mr. Cosens resigned as Dean of the Faculty to take a position with forest industry[5] and was succeeded by Professor Sisam. At the time of his appointment to the staff of the Faculty in 1934, Dr. Howe had said that in view of Mr. Cosens's well-rounded experience in forestry, in both its theoretical and its practical aspects, reinforced by a natural talent for teaching, his appointment was a fortunate one for the Faculty. This was indeed true. Soon after his appointment, the field training programme was reorganized, so that it covered a wide range of practical exercises and became a requirement for all students in each of the four years of the course. Mr. Cosens was also largely responsible for locating and acquiring under agreement the area which now constitutes the University Forest. Although no longer a member of the staff, Mr. Cosens has continued to give the Faculty his full support and has contributed most generously to its scholarship and research programme as well as to other phases of its work.

As noted in chapter VIII, with the revision of the agreement respecting the University Forest Mr. A. D. Hall[6] was appointed to the Faculty staff in charge of the management of the Forest. In 1952 Mr. Hall became Assistant Professor in charge of Wood Technology on the teaching staff in Toronto, and in 1956 Mr. N. L. Kissick[7] was appointed Manager of the University Forest with the rank of Assistant Professor.

During the two years 1952-4, Mr. G. A. Hills of the Research Division, Department of Lands and Forests, gave the undergraduate

---

Engineers and served in the United Kingdom and Europe from 1943 until he returned to Canada in 1946. He qualified for his M.F. degree at Duke University in 1951, and became Associate Professor in 1953. From October, 1954 to 1958, he served as Commanding Officer of the University contingent of the C.O.T.C., and was awarded the Canada Forces Decoration in 1954.

[5]Mr. Cosens is at present Vice-President, Woodlands, Kimberly-Clark Canada, Ltd.
[6]A. D. Hall graduated from the Faculty in 1948 and was employed with the J. J. McFadden Co. Ltd. before his appointment to the University Forest.
[7]N. L. Kissick graduated from the Faculty in 1948, and from that date to his appointment on the University staff was employed with Marathon Paper Mills of Canada, Ltd. He obtained his M.F. degree at Yale University in 1951.

56 FORESTRY EDUCATION AT TORONTO

lecture course on Forest Soils, and also offered a seminar in Forest Soil Ecology for graduate students. This work was made the responsibility of a permanent member of the Faculty staff when K. A. Armson[8] was appointed as Lecturer in 1954.

When in 1956 the Abitibi Power & Paper Company Limited established the Abitibi Chair of Forest Biology, Dr. J. L. Farrar[9] was appointed as the first incumbent.

In 1957, Professor Dwight retired and in recognition of his services to the Faculty and University was appointed by the Board of Governors Professor Emeritus of Forestry; in the same year he was made an Honorary Member of the Canadian Institute of Forestry. In addition to his teaching and research in Forest Mensuration, Professor Dwight always took a keen interest in student activities, particularly athletics; this fact was appropriately marked by the Class of 1951, when it presented to the Faculty the "T. W. Dwight Trophy" for annual award to the student contributing most during the year in athletic participation, leadership, and sportsmanship.

Professor Dwight was succeeded by F. M. Buckingham,[10] who in 1957 was appointed to the staff as Assistant Professor.

The most recent member of staff is Erik Jorgensen, who early in 1959 was appointed Assistant Professor in charge of Forest Pathology. Professor Jorgensen received his scientific training at the Royal Veterinary and Agricultural College of Copenhagen, Denmark, and for the past few years prior to his appointment on the staff of the Faculty has been engaged in research on tree diseases in forest plantations for the Division of Forest Biology of the federal Department of Agriculture.

As staff has increased, it has been possible in recent years for members to be granted leave-of-absence for the purpose of taking advanced studies elsewhere. Thus Professor Michell spent a year at

[8]K. A. Armson, a graduate of the Faculty in 1951, had subsequently been employed with the Research Division, Department of Lands and Forests. He qualified for the Diploma in Forestry at Oxford in 1955, and was appointed Assistant Professor in 1957.

[9]J. L. Farrar graduated from the Faculty in 1936, and received his Master's (1939) and Ph.D. (1955) degrees from Yale University; he had been engaged as a research forester with the federal Forestry Branch previous to his appointment with the Faculty except for the period 1941-5 when he served overseas with the R.C.A.F.

[10]F. M. Buckingham, a graduate of the University of New Brunswick (1949), who had taken his master's degree at Harvard in 1950, was on the staff of the Faculty of Forestry, University of New Brunswick, before coming to Toronto. He was appointed Associate Professor in 1960.

Duke University (1950–1), Professor Armson at Oxford (1955–6), and Professor Hall at the New York State College of Forestry (1956–7).

During this period forestry education in Ontario attained a number of its long-sought objectives, including a permanent field station readily accessible to Toronto, a forest ranger school and, most recently, greatly improved facilities for research and graduate study through provision of accommodation and facilities at Glendon Hall, an estate that had been bequeathed to the University by the late Mrs. E. R. Wood. The close association of the Faculty with the Department of Botany in developing the programme at Glendon Hall has been of special value. A more detailed treatment of these matters will be found in chapters VII and VIII.

Within the past two years, as part of the expansion programme of the University, the Forestry Building has been moved to a position about two hundred feet north of its original site, a feat that would have been beyond the imagination of those who attended the opening ceremonies in January, 1926. This move has been advantageous, for, as a result of deepening and extending the basement, accommodation has been provided for a new students' common room and facilities for a wood-testing laboratory and a dry kiln. The common room has been panelled in hardboard provided through the courtesy of the Abitibi Power & Paper Company Limited, and it has also been completely furnished through the generous gift of an early alumnus, Mr. W. J. Van Dusen, '12, of Vancouver. Other gifts that have added to the appearance of this room, as well as serving their special functions, are a trophy case given by the class of 1957 and, most recently, an electric clock given by the class of 1960.

Partly as a result of this move, the library accommodation in the Faculty has been increased by making use of the old common room in the southwest corner of the building and by removing at an earlier date the wall between the original library and the room in the northwest corner. Thus there is more space to accommodate the library collection with its indexes and catalogues and to improve access to them. The usefulness of the library has also been greatly enhanced for students and staff alike with the appointment of a full-time librarian in 1959. Furthermore, the Faculty has been fortunate in having its normal allotment for the purchase of accessions augmented, first through the fund established by the Alumni in memory of Miss Grace McAree,[11] and second through the endowment fund recently established by the Booth Lumber Company. These are both of importance, especially in making available reference documents of an historical and scientific nature that would not otherwise be available. Most welcome additions to the furniture of the library include a lectern given by the class of 1949 in memory of R. A. Smith,[12] a periodical rack given through the Grace McAree Fund, and most recently a new set of bookshelves, given by the class of 1949 in memory of R. L. Black.[12]

In 1957, celebrations to mark the fiftieth anniversary of the Faculty were attended by nearly four hundred members of the Alumni. These celebrations, which were held immediately following the 49th Annual Meeting of the Canadian Institute of Forestry, began with a dinner-dance at the Seaway Motel on the evening of October 24, and concluded with a meeting of the Alumni Association on the morning of Saturday, October 26.

Of special significance was the Convocation held on the Friday evening, when the Chancellor of the University, on behalf of the Senate, conferred the degree of Doctor of Laws, *honoris causa*, on six Canadians who had made an outstanding contribution in the forestry profession of this country: H. R. MacMillan, E. J. Zavitz, W. A. Delahey, J. M. Gibson, R. W. Lyons, and Avila Bedard. Convocation was addressed by Dr. MacMillan on the subject "The Profession and Practice of Forestry in Canada 1907–1957"(39). Just prior to Convocation, Forestry Alumni were guests of the Board of Governors of the University at a dinner given in honour of the occasion in the Great Hall, Hart House.

An important contribution to these celebrations was the Open House held at the Forestry Building and at Glendon Hall, when the students and staff were hosts to many visitors, and through exhibits and demonstrations were able to acquaint them with some aspects of the Faculty's programme.

To mark this anniversary, the forest industries of Ontario presented wood panelling of native Ontario species for the library and other rooms on the ground floor, thus greatly improving the appearance

---

[11]Secretary and Librarian, Faculty of Forestry, from 1931 until her death in 1950.
[12]Both members of the class of 1949.

of the building. Those especially responsible for this action were J. W. McNutt, '32, and C. R. Mills, '15, at the time President and Secretary Manager respectively of the Ontario Forest Industries Association.

The period under review has been one of progress in certain phases of forestry in this country. The earlier legislation relating to the sustained yield management of Ontario's forests was reviewed and consolidated in the Crown Timber Act of 1952 which provides authority through the Minister of Lands and Forests for the organization and management of the provincial Crown forests, the harvesting of timber under regulation, and the maintenance of forest land productivity. Technical developments in the use of the aeroplane and aerial photography have facilitated the collection and analysis of information with respect to these forests to provide the basis for their management, and a method of inventory survey has been developed particularly suited to the forestry conditions of the Province (10). There have been important developments in fire protection techniques and in methods of harvesting of the timber crop. Increasing attention has been given to the question of regeneration, both through the expansion of nursery facilities and planting programmes on the one hand and efforts to develop silvicultural prescriptions to assist in natural re-stocking on the other. The pressure on the forest for recreational and other uses as well as timber production has increased greatly, with the result that more emphasis is being given to the concept of multiple use of the forest resource and, as a corollary, closer coordination in the management of all natural resources within a given area. As these various demands on forest land increase, as they undoubtedly will, the work and responsibilities of the forest land manager will become even more varied and complex, and his success will depend increasingly on the adequacy of his professional education.

VI. Curriculum, Enrolment, and Employment

CURRICULUM

BECAUSE OF limited facilities and small staff, and also for reasons of practicability in meeting the needs of a new profession, the work of the Faculty in the beginning and for a good many years thereafter was confined to undergraduate education, represented primarily by the four-year course leading to the degree of Bachelor of the Science of Forestry (B.Sc.F.). The background of a curriculum for professional forestry education was discussed by Dr. Fernow in a paper (20) published in December 1907, where, after outlining the philosophy of higher education in preparing for a professional career, he describes the scope and content of the course to be presented in the Faculty of Forestry, University of Toronto. It is emphasized in that paper that the course should give the broadest professional forestry education "in order to provide a firm foundation for leadership." To this end, the early four-year curriculum[1] included a number of liberal arts subjects and provided some time for electives in the fourth year which could be used "either for specializing in various directions, or adding generally cultural subjects, or for supplementing in subjects in which the student feels himself deficient."

It was partly with the same purpose in mind that in 1909 a six-year course was offered with a broad enough coverage of arts and science to entitle the graduate to a B.A. as well as his B.Sc.F. degree. Owing perhaps to the length of time involved, the course did not attract many students and was withdrawn in 1921.

For the first few years after the Faculty was established, the curriculum was so arranged that a student might obtain preparatory training in the most essential branches of forestry by the end of the third year, the successful completion of which would entitle him to a diploma; with this he could return at any time to complete the work

[1]An outline of the original curriculum will be found in appendix IV.

for his degree.² This arrangement followed closely that in the Faculty of Applied Science and Engineering, where until the session 1910–11 the undergraduate course covered a three-year period and led to a diploma, a fourth or postgraduate year being required to qualify for the B.A.Sc. degree.³ In Forestry there is no record of a diploma being awarded, all successful candidates having completed the four-year course, thus qualifying for the degree.

Apart from degree courses, opportunity was given to mature (at least twenty-one-year-old) experienced individuals, who did not have the entrance requirements, to register as special students in order to receive some useful training in technical forestry subjects. This represented the first approach to the kind of training that would some forty years later be offered through the Forest Ranger School.

By 1911, an effort was being made to supplement the formal lecture course, which of necessity was based largely on European experience, with some account of field conditions and forestry in this country. During the next two years a series of short lecture courses was given by guest lecturers on subjects that included logging methods in eastern Canada, the work of the Dominion Forestry Branch, and diseases of forest trees, the last being given by an eminent German forester, Dr. Herman Schenck.

During this early period, up to about 1920, the curriculum was under constant review, and a number of changes were made, these being influenced not so much by developments in forestry practice as by a better understanding of Canadian forest conditions and the problems associated therewith. In a series of articles appearing in the *Canadian Forestry Magazine* that year (1920), Dean Howe gave a comprehensive account of the position reached in university education for the forester both in theory and practice, the purpose of such training, and opportunities open for graduates in this country (30).

During the 1920's, as employment became more diversified with an increasing demand for foresters in industry, further consideration was given to curriculum requirements. Among the suggestions made at that time, principally by Alumni, were (i) that practice camp be

---

[2]This arrangement was authorized under Senate Statute 585 of May 13, 1907, and was replaced by the present four-year degree course under Statute 650 of June 27, 1910.

[3]The present four-year undergraduate course leading to the B.A.Sc. degree was established in the session 1909–10 (15).

extended in time to cover the entire summer at the end of the second year, (ii) that the summer prior to admission into the Faculty be spent by the candidates in the field studying surveying, dendrology, and mensuration, and (iii) that the general four-year undergraduate course be reorganized so as to offer a common curriculum in the first and second years with opportunity in the third and fourth years to specialize either in the biological subjects basic to silviculture, or engineering and related subjects of importance to logging. Nothing came of these suggestions at the time, and the next development of importance occurred in 1931–2, when, as a result of efforts to increase the practicality of the course, a series of lectures was given by industrial foresters, including R. W. Lyons, '15, and the late Ellwood Wilson.[4]

These lectures and the discussions associated with them stimulated considerable interest in the curriculum and its adequacy to meet the needs of the profession at that time. As a result, in November 1931 a questionnaire was circulated to all Alumni, asking for suggestions towards improving its technical or professional content.

This questionnaire and the replies it brought forth were discussed by Dr. Howe in a paper delivered before the annual meeting of the Canadian Society of Forest Engineers in 1932 (*31*). He pointed out that four general propositions had been suggested to the Alumni: a six-year course (combined engineering and forestry); a five-year course with emphasis on engineering or biological subjects in the fifth year; a four-year course with a division at the end of the second year, one part specializing in biological subjects and the other in engineering subjects;[5] and the maintenance of the four-year course essentially as it was at that time with some additions and subtractions. Replies were received from 80 per cent of those to whom the questionnaire was sent, and these showed that 33 per cent favoured a division of the four-year course at the end of the second year, 20 per cent wished to maintain the pattern of the existing course, though with some change in subject content, 23 per cent favoured the five-year course, and 14 per cent the six-year course.

In commenting on this report, A. Koroleff (*35*) suggested that there was a need to reorient the programme of training for those

[4]As noted in chapter IV, this pattern was continued in 1932–3, when, following the resignation of Professor Millar, a series of special lectures in Forest Protection and Utilization was given by foresters from industry and government.

[5]As had been proposed five years earlier.

CURRICULUM, ENROLMENT, AND EMPLOYMENT 63

men intending to go into industrial forestry. Among the points emphasized were the need for students to be familiar with forest conditions, if they were to make the best use of their training; for the industrial forester, "a more substantial knowledge as applied to logging and logging techniques . . . [and] a greater understanding of finance and woods accounting"; and the need to stress the interrelation of logging and silviculture. On this last point, Koroleff emphasized the lack of understanding and co-operation often existing between students of silviculture and industrial foresters, and brought out the need for a common course in silviculture and logging, this being an obvious line of development, as in most cases it would be only through logging operations that silvicultural techniques could be applied. Other speakers at this meeting emphasized the importance of certain engineering and business subjects in the training of foresters for industrial work (9, 34) and also the need for graduates to have a period of in-service training under proper supervision in order to gain useful experience and be better qualified in logging (24).

While discussions taking place and resolutions passed at the annual meeting of the C.S.F.E. cannot properly be considered as a part of the history of the Faculty, nevertheless the discussion referred to above and the following resolution, to which it led, are recorded here, as they are both related in no small measure to the curriculum study being carried on in the Faculty at Toronto at that time. The resolution passed at the 1932 annual meeting of the C.S.F.E. (55) stated, "that while maintaining the necessity for a thorough training in the fundamentals of forestry, and while suggesting the avoidance of the trade school idea in forestry education, yet we urge a broadening of the training in such subjects as engineering, logging, and utilization in our forestry schools, and we especially urge greater provision for undergraduate students in forestry to gain practical experience in the woods through employment by the pulp and paper and other wood-using industries."

After a careful evaluation of the replies to the questionnaire sent out by the Faculty and a detailed study of the whole matter by members of the staff, it was decided to retain the four-year general course, with the following subjects added in 1933 as reported by Professor Hosie in the *News Letter* for that year: Calculus and Analytical Geometry better to qualify the student for applied forestry mathematics and postgraduate studies; Hydraulics, directed particularly to the needs of the industrial forester on problems associated with the water transportation of wood; Forest Description to facilitate the study, description, and reporting on forest conditions; and English, for the reason no doubt that professional competence rests largely on the ability of the individual to express himself in clear, concise language. A little later, in 1936, probably as a result of the increasing interest in all phases of resource management associated with the forests, a course in Fish and Wildlife Management was introduced, first on a half-credit basis, but later extended to a full, one-lecture subject; and to add to the practical qualifications of the graduate, a field course in scaling was introduced in the same year, this work to be given during the spring camp period by members of the staff of the Department of Lands and Forests.

Also during this period, as a result of the increasing competition that forest products were meeting in construction and associated industries, it was urged that more attention be given to the study of wood as an industrial material and to the means for improving its usefulness and marketability. A resolution was passed at the annual meeting of the Canadian Society of Forest Engineers in 1934, drawing the attention of the Canadian forestry schools "to the desirability of giving greater attention to utilization in curricula adopted as being in accord with the best interests of the profession under present economic conditions in Canada" (40). In the same year, it was suggested by Dean Howe in the *News Letter* that one of the greatest needs of the Faculty was a specialist in wood utilization, whose function would be to study new uses and new markets for wood products as a background for giving instruction and developing some research in this field. It was not possible to add to the staff at the time, and while the programme in timber physics and technology was expanded a little in order to make the forestry student more knowledgeable in this field, no attempt was made to train specialists in wood technology. It was recognized that this would be a major undertaking, for which neither staff nor facilities were available; it was also recognized that the general field of wood technology and forest products represents one of a number of broad areas of applied science which when treated within clearly defined limits can contribute much to the education of a forester as such—specialization in these subjects, however, usually requires the setting up of a separate division or department within the University.

The needs of the wood-using industries for qualified technical assistance was again considered at the annual meeting of the Canadian Society of Forest Engineers in 1944, and a resolution was passed recommending that a study be made of the possibility of serving those needs by setting up a university course combining certain aspects of forestry and engineering. At Toronto, this was followed by the establishment of the Canadian Lumbermen's Association Fellowship to support a graduate in either forestry or engineering who wished to take advanced work in timber physics.[6]

In forest protection, mainly as a result of successive infestations in epidemic proportions of the spruce budworm and spruce sawfly in the pulpwood forests of eastern Canada, it was strongly urged that more emphasis be given to the teaching of forest entomology, and to this end it was suggested by some people that the undergraduate course be divided after the second year, so that students who wished to do so could specialize in this field at the undergraduate level. As with the earlier proposals to divide the curriculum midway through the course, no action was taken on this matter at Toronto, it being the view that such specialization should be undertaken at the postgraduate level only. Subsequently, Dr. C. E. Atwood was appointed as forest entomologist in the Department of Zoology with responsibility for supervising work in this field for the University.

As noted elsewhere, a marked increase of emphasis on forestry and resource conservation in general developed during the late thirties and early forties, partly as a result of improved economic conditions, perhaps partly because of the conservation developments that had taken place in the United States, and partly, during the war, through the great increase in demand for wood and the planning for post-war reconstruction of the nation's economy. This trend inevitably led to a further review of forestry school curricula at the national level, in particular at the annual meeting of C.S.F.E. in 1946 when a good deal of time was devoted to the discussion of forestry education in Canada; out of this came a resolution to consider undertaking a survey

[6] Four graduates in engineering have held this fellowship; their names and the titles of the theses submitted for their graduate degrees are as follows:
W. Thornber: "Glued Wood Joints"
R. H. Harrison: "Developments in the Structural Use of Wood"
S. P. Fox: "An Investigation into the Effects of Certain Variables in Scarf-jointed Timber Laminations"
E. D. Turnbull: "An Investigation into the Stresses Developed within the Plies of Plywood Box-beams under Load."

of the entire forest education field in this country (56), somewhat along the lines of that undertaken by Graves and Guise in the United States some years earlier (27). So far, this suggestion has not been implemented.

No further changes were made in the course of study at the Toronto Faculty up to 1948 when a review of the content in relation to apparent needs was begun by the staff, this being completed in 1953. As a result, certain changes and additions were recommended to and approved by the Senate of the University with the following objectives in mind:

(i) To provide more adequately for field training, first by increasing the period of spring field work at the end of each year from three to four weeks, and second by requiring as part of this programme that each student collect, compile, and analyse all relevant data for a selected block on the University Forest, and from these data prepare a plan of management. The purpose of this project would be twofold: to give the student practical field and office experience in the preparation of a forest management plan, and also to afford an opportunity to co-ordinate all the various phases of forestry and thus on a small scale establish their interrelation and interdependence.

(ii) To broaden the basis of what is essentially a professional course by giving more emphasis to subjects of general educational importance. To this end, courses in the Philosophy of Science and Modern History were added to the curriculum in place of subjects that were considered less important or obsolete.

(iii) To give some recognition at the undergraduate level to the diversity of interests within the field of forestry and make it possible for the individual to study a little more extensively in the field of his particular interest. Accordingly, a number of optional subjects were introduced in the fourth-year curriculum, the minimum time devoted to these being equivalent to two hours of lectures and a laboratory period per week.

These changes and additions were made and have been in effect for the past seven years. A further study of course content has just been completed by a committee of the staff, and on the basis of its recommendations, approved by the Faculty Council, certain other changes, mainly of emphasis, are being made at the present time.

In view of some of the recommendations that have been made in the past with respect to curriculum changes, it is perhaps worth noting that in reviews that have been made from time to time over the years most staff members have invariably favoured the general, non-specialized type of course; it is felt that this gives the student a broad training, fits him for general forestry practice, and provides him with the necessary background for further study at the postgraduate level when, after a certain amount of practical experience, he should be better able to select the field in which to specialize.

Forestry is essentially an applied science and university education must be strongly supported by field experience. It is, therefore, of some significance that during the four-year undergraduate course the students receive a wide range of practical demonstration and experience, including fifteen weeks at the University Forest, a week at a provincial station studying plantation management and nursery work, a week on a logging operation in northern Ontario, visits to fifteen or twenty mills and wood-manufacturing plants in southern Ontario, three visits arranged by the Department of Lands and Forests to see in successive years a fire protection headquarters, a management unit, and a research station, and finally employment in the woods for all undergraduates during three summer vacation periods. In recent years through the assistance of the Department of Lands and Forests and forest industries, it has been possible once more for third-year students to visit logging operations as a group under the supervision of the member of staff in charge of this subject.

In connection with the undergraduate programme in the Faculty, it is of interest to note the various scholarships, prizes, and other awards that have been established from time to time for competition in each of the four years of the course. A list of these presently available, with the names of the donors and terms of award, is given in appendix v.

ADMISSION REQUIREMENTS

Academic requirements for admission to a university course may be evaluated in terms of (*a*) the function they serve, for example, in providing for subjects that are prerequisite to the professional course, and (*b*) the standard or level of attainment specified in relation to the standard of the university as a whole and the requirements of the profession. In the beginning, the Faculty of Forestry required Junior Matriculation (or its equivalent) in English, history, mathematics, German, and either French or Latin with honour standing in English and mathematics (44). This was relatively high at the time, it being the aim, according to Dean Fernow, (a) to keep registration within the bounds of probable employment opportunities, and (b) to try to limit candidates to those likely to give leadership to the profession after graduation.

Periodically, these requirements have been raised in keeping with the general trend in the University. In his annual report for 1920, Dr. Howe recommended that the entrance requirements should be raised to Senior Matriculation. This was done in 1923, which may account in part for the marked reduction in the number entering the Faculty in the following year. At first the Senior Matriculation subjects were English, mathematics (algebra, trigonometry, and geometry), and a foreign language. Subsequently, two of the four sciences were added to these.

In recent years there has been a general raising of University admission requirements, and at the present time those for the Faculty of Forestry are an average of sixty per cent[7] or better for the Senior Matriculation papers in English (2), mathematics (3), science (2),[8] and a foreign language (2).

ENROLMENT AND EMPLOYMENT

The growth of the Faculty of Forestry may be measured in many ways, one of the more significant being the number of first-year students enrolling each year, and as a corollary of that, the number of graduates. In the table given in appendix II, annual figures are listed and combined for successive decades to show the enrolment of graduate students, undergraduates in each year of the course, special or occasional students, and the numbers of those graduating with a B.Sc.F. degree.

From the time the Faculty was established, when the profession was hardly known and the demand for graduates barely existed, there has

[7]This average is the minimum required for admission to any degree course in the University at the present time.

[8]Beginning in the fall of 1960, the two sciences, physics and chemistry, are required without option.

been a steady improvement and expansion of opportunity for employment in forestry. Conditions and factors that have brought this about include (a) progressive changes in government policy and legislation with respect to the management of natural resources, (b) the contribution the graduates themselves have made in the administration and development of these resources, (c) the economic expansion that has taken place in Canada, particularly in recent years.

Parallel with these developments, there has been a gradual over-all increase in student enrolment, though from time to time there have been marked fluctuations in this trend caused, for example, by wartime conditions, sharp changes in the economy of the country (and opportunity for employment), and academic requirements for admission to the Faculty. Thus the raising of these requirements in 1923 to the Senior Matriculation standard, and in 1954 to an average of third class honours or better (Senior Matriculation), was followed in each case by a marked reduction for one year at least in the number of students being admitted to the first year.

War conditions influenced not only the number of men enrolling in the first year, but even more markedly, for the time being, the number of those graduating, as in both world wars a high proportion of the undergraduate students enlisted before the completion of their course. The effect of this is shown in the number of those graduating in the years 1917–18–19 and 1944 and 1945. Fortunately, in each case a good many of these undergraduates were able to return and take their degree after the cessation of hostilities.

High enrolment from 1927 to 1933 probably reflected the rapid expansion in the pulp and paper industry and the progress that was being made at that time in forest policy by the Ontario Government and the consequent increased opportunities for employment. The high enrolment of 1945–7, when the majority of first-year students were ex-service men, probably resulted in part from government financial assistance in making it possible to go to university at all, in part from what these men had seen of forestry in Europe and the outdoor life to which they had grown accustomed there, and in part from suggestions made by army rehabilitation officers. These latter were influenced quite rightly by the urgent need for foresters in both industry and government to deal with current problems, and by the progress that had apparently been made during the war years by both federal and provincial governments towards a more positive approach in resource management.

With the heavy enrolment of ex-service men during the period 1945–7, the number of candidates admitted direct from high school had to be restricted. However, by 1948 this was no longer necessary, and in that year the Faculty had the highest first-year registration of secondary school students ever recorded—a reflection once again of employment opportunities favoured by forestry development in both government services and industry.

Of the 840 graduates of the Faculty, by far the majority (726) come from the Province of Ontario. Those not from Ontario (114) represent as their places of origin each of the other provinces—the largest numbers coming from the adjacent provinces of Quebec (16) and Manitoba (14)—and Great Britain (17), the United States (7), the British West Indies (6), and northwestern Europe (27).

One may ask, what of the future trend in undergraduate enrolment? At the present time in this country, the profession is just completing its first half-century of practice. With more graduates taking positions of executive and administrative responsibility and with an increasing interest and concern being shown in matters affecting the development of our natural resources, there seems every reason to expect a continuing increase in the demand for graduates in forestry with a comparable growth in the undergraduate population.

Undoubtedly the rate of increase will accelerate as we become more dependent on the managed forest for our timber supplies. Furthermore, the solution of problems associated with more intensive management will require, more than in the past, the training of men as specialists in those fields where the need for research is most urgent. This in turn should lead to greater emphasis on, and support for, programmes of research and graduate study in this and other faculties of forestry in the country.

Taking into consideration the facilities available in the Faculty and the employment pattern as it is presently developing, a maximum registration of 150 undergraduate students has been set as the limit for the next few years, though undoubtedly there will be a further increase later on. It should be noted that this registration target takes into account the increasing number of forest technicians becoming available through the ranger schools across the country.⁹ These men are qualified to do much of the routine field and office work associated with forestry undertakings; in those European countries where forestry is well advanced, the ratio of technicians to professional foresters is about 4 to 1.

⁹Schools in Canada responsible for the training of rangers or forest technicians at the present time are as follows:
L'Ecole forestière, Duchesnay, P.Q.
Maritime Forest Ranger School, Fredericton, N.B.
Ontario Forest Ranger School, Dorset, Ont.
British Columbia Forest Ranger School, New Westminster, B.C.
Lakehead College of Arts, Science, & Technology, Fort William, Ont.
Saskatchewan Forest Ranger School, Prince Albert, Sask.

VII. Graduate Studies and Research

DURING THE EARLY years of the Faculty, there was little opportunity to provide for postgraduate training, and indeed the demand for advanced degrees in forestry was slight, owing perhaps to the fact that initially all foresters were engaged in work of an extensive nature—the carrying out of reconnaissance surveys, developing more effective fire protection, and setting up administrative organizations.

The professional degree of Forest Engineer (F.E.) had been offered from the time the Faculty was first established,[1] this being granted to a graduate forester who, after three years' employment in professional work, submitted to the University an acceptable thesis on an approved subject; nine such degrees have been granted. In 1952 this degree was withdrawn, as it was felt that all credits given by the Faculty through the School of Graduate Studies should be based on a programme of academic study and scientific research, first at the master's level and later, as conditions permit, to include the Ph.D.

In the early stages of forestry development, members of the Faculty staff were involved in the planning and initiation of research programmes for both federal and provincial governments. Thus during the period 1917–21, Dr. Howe was responsible for a research programme under the Commission of Conservation and in co-operation with various pulp and paper companies and provincial governments, the main purpose being to study problems of regeneration and growth associated with the continuous productivity of pulpwood lands. In the meantime, the first comprehensive plan for carrying on silvicultural research in Canada was outlined in a report prepared by Professor Millar for the Dominion Forest Service in 1915. War delayed its implementation, but as reported by Professor Dwight (13), the federal programme was under way by 1922, with the Forestry

---

[1]When in March, 1922, the Senate established the School of Graduate Studies, this degree (F.E.) was among those placed under the jurisdiction of the School.

Branch having taken over the work of the Commission of Conservation, which was dissolved in 1921.

During the period 1927–32, three members of the Faculty worked each summer on projects for the Ontario Government under the direction of the Advisory Board.[2] However, despite these developments, and the fact that as early as 1920 Dr. Howe had stated adequate provision for postgraduate training should be one of the main objectives of forestry education in Ontario,[3] the programme for such training in the Faculty developed very slowly. The first candidate, Gordon G. Cosens, '23, began his studies in 1926 and received the degree, Master of Arts, in 1927. He was followed by R. C. Hosie who received his M.A. in 1929. All subsequent candidates have received the degree, Master of the Science of Forestry, which was formally established by the Council of the School of Graduate Studies on March 19, 1931. Undoubtedly the programme of research and postgraduate training that was contemplated for the Faculty and had just got under way at that time would have gone ahead more rapidly but for the economic depression and the Second World War. However, the trend thus interrupted was resumed about 1945, when some University funds were allocated to the Faculty for research purposes and studies were initiated on the University Forest.

In a review of the Faculty's work given before the Senate of the University in the spring of 1950, Dean Sisam pointed out that owing to the difficulties during the earlier period only six candidates had completed the requirements for their master's degree up to that time, and suggested that one of the main objectives of the Faculty in the years ahead should be "to increase and improve the opportunities for postgraduate training, particularly in the biological aspects of forestry." Fortunately, assistance to meet this objective was forthcoming almost immediately, as in 1951 the University made available to the Faculty of Forestry and the Department of Botany a part of the Glendon Hall estate for use as a research centre. For the first few years the programme at Glendon Hall could develop only gradually and, apart from the plant itself, was dependent in large measure on support

[2] See p. 39.
[3] Dean Howe, in his 1920 report to the President of the University, stated that plans were under way to provide "postgraduate courses in such subjects as forest administration, forest mensuration, forest protection, forest ecology, forest fungology."

received from outside sources including Alumni, the University of Toronto Associates, Inc., New York, and the Ontario Research Council. In 1956, the value of the Glendon Hall unit was greatly enhanced with the establishment by the Abitibi Power & Paper Company Limited of a research professorship in forest biology. More recently, important pieces of equipment for use in this laboratory have been provided by the Abitibi Company, the Canadian International Paper Company, and the Ontario Research Foundation, while others have been made available on loan by the Department of Lands and Forests. During the past year, as the bulk of the Glendon Hall property has been transferred to York University, a small area on the south side was retained by the University of Toronto, and here new laboratories, the greenhouse, and a nursery have been established which at present provide adequate accommodation for the forestry research programme.

Research projects being undertaken at Glendon Hall are mainly fundamental ones in forest ecology and tree physiology, dealing particularly with light and water relations and mineral nutrition, while at the University Forest work is more immediately practical and in the fields of silviculture, utilization, and logging.

As efforts have been made to expand the graduate programme in the Faculty, it has become increasingly apparent that one of the critical factors is the provision of financial assistance for graduate students. Some progress has been made in this direction through grants from the University, the Ontario Research Foundation (and earlier the Ontario Research Council), and the Associates of the University of Toronto Inc. In addition, the following graduate fellowships have been established:

(i) The Canadian Lumbermen's Association Timber Research Fellowship (1945–).
(ii) The Spruce Falls Power and Paper Company Limited Research Fellowships (1948–1955).
(iii) The Toronto Anglers' and Hunters' Association Fellowships in Forest Soils (1956–) and Forest Management (1958–).
(iv) Kimberly-Clark Corporation of Canada Limited Fellowship in Silviculture (1958–).
(v) Two Fellowships for advanced study and research in Forest Economics (1956–).

At present, graduate courses, administered by the School of

GRADUATE STUDIES AND RESEARCH 75

Graduate Studies, are offered at the master's level in the main branches of forestry. The following is a list of all postgraduate degrees that have been awarded since the establishment of the Faculty:

Name	Date	Degree	Title of thesis
Kynoch, W.	1918	F.E.	An Investigation of the Adaptability of Jack Pine and Eastern Hemlock to Preservative Treatment with Creosote Oil
Connell, A. B.	1925	F.E.	The Forest Types of Eastern Saskatchewan
Wright, W. G.	1925	F.E.	Taper as a Factor in the Measurement of Standing Timber
Cosens, G. G.	1927	M.A.	(Through examination)
Hosie, R. C.	1929	M.A.	A Study of the Indicator Significance of the Ground Vegetation as a Basis in the Classification of Forest Types
Millar, J. B.	1936	M.Sc.F.	The Silvicultural Characteristics of Black Spruce in the Clay Belt of Northern Ontario
Seheult, L. R.	1936	M.Sc.F.	The Use of Trucks in Logging Operations
Bonner, E.	1941	M.Sc.F.	Balsam Fir in the Clay Belt of Northern Ontario
Bedell, G. H. D.	1944	F.E.	A Management Plan for the Duck Mountain Forest Reserve
Brodie, J. A.	1945	M.Sc.F.	Vegetation and Soil as a Basis for the Classification of Forest Types in Ontario
Richardson, A. H.	1945	F.E.	The Ganaraska Watershed: A Study in Land Use
Catto, A. T.	1947	F.E.	Truck Roads for Woods Operations Portaging in Northwestern Quebec
Silversides, C. R.	1948	F.E.	Measuring and Determining Diameter Growth
Yuan, Tung-Kung	1950	M.Sc.F.	The Use of Flumes in the Water Transportation of Forest Products
Buckley, E. H.	1950	M.Sc.F.	Methods of Studying Height Growth and Stocking Indexes for Pure Even-aged Stands
Turner, K. B.	1950	M.Sc.F.	The Relation of Forest Composition to the Mortality of Balsam Fir Caused by the Spruce Budworm in the Algoma Forest of Ontario
Harkness, W. D.	1951	F.E.	Mechanized Operations—a Graphic Analysis of the Effect of Major Operating Factors on Actual and Potential Performance
Bayly, G. H.	1951	M.Sc.F.	A Survey of Forest-Tree Planting on Private Land in Part of Southern Ontario
Hess, Q. F.	1952	F.E.	Forest Fire Control Planning for the Province of Ontario
Schmitt, D. M.	1952	M.Sc.F.	Initial Early Root Development in Black Spruce
Wilkes, G. C.	1952	M.Sc.F.	Taxation of the Forest Industries of Ontario

Name	Date	Degree	Title of thesis
Andrews, G. W. V.	1952	M.Sc.F.	The Taxation of Privately Owned Woodlands under the Municipal System of Southern Ontario
Jameson, J. S.	1953	M.Sc.F.	An Investigation into the Productivity of Three Physiographic Sites in the Cochrane District of Ontario
Collict, F. T.	1953	M.Sc.F.	Some of the Economic Aspects of Sustained Yield Forestry
Grant, J. A. C.	1954	M.Sc.F.	The Effect of Length of Day on Tree Seedlings
Larsson, H. C.	1955	M.Sc.F.	The Effect of Different Water Treatments on Seedling Survival
Loucks, O. L.	1955	M.Sc.F.	A Study of Lakeshore Reservations of Pine, Quetico Provincial Park, Ont.
Carmichael, A. J.	1956	M.Sc.F.	Determination of the Maximum Air Temperature Tolerated by Red Pine, Jack Pine, White Spruce and Black Spruce Seeds at Low Relative Humidities
Dixon, M. M.	1956	M.Sc.F.	An Appraisal of Present Hauling Trends in the Northern Clay Belt
Drysdale, D. P.	1957	M.Sc.F.	A Study of the Forest Industry of Simcoe County and the Factors Relating to Its Present and Future Importance in That Economy
Grinnell, W. R.	1957	M.Sc.F.	The Management of Small Forest Areas in Southern Ontario
Salm, J.	1959	M.Sc.F.	A Review of Current Forest Nursery Practice
Protich, G.	1959	M.Sc.F.	Study of Forest Management Techniques Applicable to the University of Toronto Forest
Steneker, G. A.	1960	M.Sc.F.	Increment of Advanced Growth of Sugar Maple Following Release
Gupta, M.	1960	M.Sc.F.	Relationships of Moisture Regime and Texture Depth Index with the Site Index for Black Spruce in the Boreal Forests of Ontario
Evert, F.	1960	M.Sc.F.	Forest Survey Methods based on Aerial Photographs

It should be noted that in addition to the programme of postgraduate studies being carried on within the Faculty of Forestry, work at both the M.A. and Ph.D. levels has been given over a number of years to graduates in Forestry and Honour Science by the Departments of Botany and Zoology, Faculty of Arts, in the fields of forest pathology and forest entomology respectively.

With the provision that has so far been made of staff, plant, equipment, and student assistance, and having in mind the very real need for men with specialized training to handle many of the detailed

GRADUATE STUDIES AND RESEARCH 77

and complex problems associated with more intensive forest management, it is expected that in the years ahead there will be a considerable further expansion in the programme of research and graduate studies.

To provide for the publication of the results of research within the Faculty (apart from those appearing in the periodical literature) and the papers presented by guest lecturers, two series, one of forestry bulletins and the other of technical reports, have been established. The titles and authors of works published in these series up to the present time are as follows:

FORESTRY BULLETINS

No. 1. *The Relationship between Stocking and Size of Quadrat*, by J. A. C. GRANT, 1951.
No. 2. *Forest Regeneration in Ontario*, by R. C. HOSIE, 1953.
No. 3. *Taxation of the Forest Industries in Ontario*, by G. C. WILKES, 1954.
No. 4. *Forest Hygiene in Great Britain*, by W. R. DAY, 1955.
No. 5. *Some Aspects of Forestry Research in Great Britain*, by L. LEYTON, 1958.
No. 6. *White Spruce Seedlings: The Growth and Seasonal Absorption of Nitrogen, Phosphorus, and Potassium*, by K. A. ARMSON, 1960.

TECHNICAL REPORTS

No. 1. *An Example of the Effect of Past Use of Land on Fertility Levels and Growth of Norway Spruce (Picea abies L. Karst.)*, K. A. ARMSON, 1959.
No. 2. *Area Measurement by Weight, A Useful Technique in Forest Inventory*, F. M. BUCKINGHAM, 1959.

VIII. University Forest and Ranger School

AS HAS BEEN mentioned earlier, the fall practice camp was held at Achray in Algonquin Park for a number of years, beginning in 1924. The main drawbacks of this location were its distance from Toronto and the lack of any definite agreement with the Department of Lands and Forests to permit long-term development. During the Achray period, the camp was held for a period of six weeks beginning about September 1, and only the fourth-year students were required to attend. This had the disadvantage that first-, second-, and third-year students received little practical field training apart from surveying before going to their summer work. In order to improve this situation, it was decided in 1935 that the first-year students should spend two weeks on field work immediately following the annual examinations in the spring, and arrangements were made with C. H. Irwin, '22,[1] for them to stay at Sherwood Forest Camp just north of Carnarvon, Ontario. So successful was the first spring camp that in the following year the period was increased to three weeks, and the students of first, second, and third years were required to attend. With this change, the need for fall practice camp for fourth-year students disappeared, and in 1937 it was discontinued, the last one being held at Sherwood Forest Camp in 1936. Subsequently the spring camp period was further extended, so that at the present time first-, second-, and third-year students have four weeks and fourth-year students three weeks of field training each year, beginning about April 15.

Although the Achray location had certain disadvantages as a permanent site for undergraduate field training, nevertheless for the time being it served its purpose well, and many students of that period will recall with considerable pleasure their fall camp experience, from the time they arrived, usually in the middle of the night, searching for "a long, low building across the track," until the day, some weeks later, when having completed their field work and visited the Petawawa Experiment Station and other points of interest in the region, the camp broke up in the vicinity of Pembroke.

[1]Owner and Director of Sherwood Forest Camp.

Sherwood Forest Camp, to which the move was made in 1935, could not itself provide a permanent field station, and so with the full support of University authorities steps were taken to locate a suitable area that would be representative of typical forest conditions and within a reasonable distance of Toronto. The area finally selected is in Haliburton County about 150 miles north of Toronto, and as at present constituted includes some 17,000 acres located in the townships of Hindon, Ridout, Sherborne, and Stanhope on both sides of Highway 35 and extending about eight miles south of Raven Lake.

It was largely through the efforts of Gordon Cosens, as a member of the Faculty staff, that in 1940 the first steps were taken towards acquiring this property; in that year six lots were purchased outright by the University, and, with the approval of the Department of Lands and Forests, cutting rights on a block of 2,871 acres of Crown land, mainly in Sherborne Township, were assigned to the University by the Royal Bank of Canada. While the assignment of rights under the licence for this land was filed with the Department of Lands and Forests, no new licence was issued to the University, but instead an Agreement was entered into between the University and the Department, dated June 27, 1944. At the time, the Department added an area of 2,130 acres of adjoining unalienated Crown lands.

In the terms of the Agreement between the University and the Department, the ownership of all but the six lots purchased by the University are to remain in the Crown, and the University accepts responsibility for the management of the property. Subsequently, contiguous areas of Crown forest were added by the Department, particularly to the west, east, and southeast of the original blocks, these being incorporated in the University Forest under the terms of the Agreement and bringing the total area of the Forest to 18,500 acres.

The region represented by the University Forest is rugged and typical of the Precambrian Shield in central Ontario.[2] The forest is of the white pine–tolerant hardwood type, and contains stands representative of the main commercial tree species to be found in Ontario, the most common for the region being white and red pine, hemlock, balsam fir, white spruce, hard maple, white and yellow birch, and red oak. As in most of this region, the University Forest was heavily cut over

[2]An interesting account of the early history of this region has been written by Dr. W. R. Haddow, '23 (28).

for white and red pine, hemlock, and the better quality hardwoods during the period 1880–1930. For some time to come, its management will be concerned mainly with the rehabilitation of portions that are inadequately stocked or stocked with species of poor quality and low value. This programme is being implemented gradually, the costs being met from returns on current timber sales.

The Agreement between the University and the Department of Lands and Forests was revised in 1950 and again in 1960, the most recent revision incorporating a ten-year operating plan which is an integral part of the long-term management plan for the Forest and is being used currently as a guide and control for all cutting and improvement operations. Also, under the present Agreement a network of access roads is being built on the Forest at the rate of about three miles per year, the annual cost not to exceed $15,000, to be borne one-third by the University, one-third by the Department of Lands and Forests, and one-third by the annual income from the Forest.

While the training of sub-professional forestry personnel and the provision of accommodation and staff to carry out this work may not be considered a University responsibility, the importance of providing men qualified to undertake many of the routine operations involved in forestry work was early recognized by the Faculty. In his report to the Royal Commission on University Finances of 1920, (52) Dr. Howe mentioned this type of school as one of the four major requirements of forestry education in Ontario, and again in 1927, the Forestry Board recommended that the government take steps to organize a forest ranger school for the purpose of training subordinate officers in the various technical aspects of forestry work.

Fifteen years later the question was again raised, this time by Peter McEwen, '16, district and regional forester at Sudbury, who in January, 1943 (three years after the University Forest had been established), presented a paper entitled "Forest Fire Protection in Post-War Rehabilitation" (37) at the annual meeting of the Canadian Society of Forest Engineers. In this paper, Mr. McEwen suggested that a training programme for demobilized personnel be established that would "develop into a permanent training school for Forest Rangers." The Department of Lands and Forests decided to act in the matter, and chose as the site for the new school the northwest shore of Lake St. Nora, just east of Highway 35 in the centre of the University Forest. As early as 1921, when carrying out a reconnaissance survey in the region, Mr. McEwen had noted that this site was particularly well suited for a Chief Ranger's headquarters or similar development.

The suitability of the site, together with the fact that the University Forest was being developed primarily for instructional purposes, led to the decision to locate the ranger school there. In the Agreement of June 27, 1944, the Department undertook to construct and operate the school and to name a director to be in charge, the buildings of the school to be used "in connection with the instruction of undergraduate and graduate students of the University for such periods and at such times as may be arranged." Mr. McEwen was appointed director of the school in the fall of 1943 with the responsibility of planning and supervising the building programme. Thus was established a cooperative project between the Department and the University that has been mutually beneficial and in this respect fulfils the aim of the Royal Commission of 1906, which, in speaking of the proposed Faculty of Forestry, suggested that its success would depend in large measure on the co-operation and support of the Department of Lands (as it was then called).

In the meantime, field instruction for the students of the Faculty was continued for a number of years at Sherwood Forest Camp. Although the first building of the Ranger School was completed in 1945, accommodation sufficient for all undergraduates was not available until 1950, and up to 1953 the third-year course in scaling was still given at Sherwood Forest Camp.

Instruction of the ranger staff of the Department preceded the building of the School; thus during the period 1941–5, at the request of the Minister of Lands and Forests, seven members of this staff were registered as occasional students in the University, each for a period of two years, and completed successfully the courses assigned to them. Also, during the same period the Faculty agreed to organize and admininister *pro tem* a course of instruction for selected groups of rangers. The first course was given at Sherwood Forest Camp in two parts, one in September 1943, and the second in September 1944. In this the Faculty was assisted by two members of the staff of the Department—Messrs. J. D. Pennock and A. J. Dunne. The Faculty staff continued to assist with this course for a few more years, but by 1953 it was acting mainly in an advisory capacity. In the meantime, ranger instructors of the staff of the Department of Lands and Forests were being trained, and gradually took over the work. During the session 1947–8, at the request of the Minister, four of these men[3] registered in the University as occasional students to receive instruction in the subjects for which they were to be responsible. At present, the Ranger School has a staff of four full-time instructors under J. L. Mennill, '48, who succeeded Mr. McEwen as Director in 1954. The Director receives assistance from an advisory council whose members represent the forest industries, the Department of Lands and Forests, and the University.

The course given at the School for forest rangers, conservation officers, and other technical personnel, covers a period of 33 weeks (3 terms of 11 weeks) within a calendar year. Intended in the first instance for the training of men employed by the Department of Lands and Forests and forest industries of the Province, the general course is now being made available to other suitably qualified applicants.

Under the 1950 revision of the Agreement between the University and the Department of Lands and Forests, the University undertook to appoint a member of the staff of the Faculty of Forestry to be resident manager of the University Forest and to assist with instruction at the Ranger School, his salary to be paid half by the University and half by the Department. From 1950 to 1952, A. D. Hall, '48, held this position, and was succeeded in 1956 by N. L. Kissick, '48 (there being no appointment for the intervening period).

The accommodation and facilities provided by the Ranger School have greatly increased the usefulness of the University Forest as a centre for field training and research. As noted above, forestry students now spend three weeks to a month there at the end of each academic year; this provides the opportunity for undertaking a variety of field exercises, including the preparation of a detailed management plan for one block of the Forest. The University also makes use of the area in field work for students from the School of Architecture and the Department of Civil Engineering.

In 1954, Dean Sisam, at the request of Mr. F. A. MacDougall, Deputy Minister of Lands and Forests, prepared a report (54) on

[3]These were A. J. Dunne, E. Goodman, J. Ruxton, and W. J. Stinson.

the Forest Ranger School, in which he reviewed its history and made a number of recommendations with regard to its future development, particularly where this might affect the interests of both the Department and the University.

From the time of its establishment, the University Forest has been used increasingly for research purposes by the Faculty, by the Department's research division, and by the Division of Forestry Biology, Department of Agriculture, Ottawa. In 1947, the Division of Forest Biology began a study of decays found in hard maple and the fungi associated therewith. This programme was gradually expanded until in 1952 a laboratory was built to the east of the Ranger School to serve as a headquarters for the study of forest pathology problems in the general region represented by the University Forest. The regional research unit of the Department of Lands and Forests is located permanently at the Ranger School. In addition to research being done by these three groups, co-operative studies have been undertaken by the Faculty in association with the Forestry Branch and the Forest Products Laboratories of the Department of Northern Affairs and National Resources,[4] and with the Ontario Agricultural College.

In addition to the University Forest, the Department of Lands and Forests has recently made available to the Faculty an area of some seventy acres representing in part a natural hardwood stand and in part open land in the process of being afforested. This area, situated within fifteen miles of Toronto, affords excellent facilities as a field laboratory for day-to-day work in connection with certain courses in forest botany, soils, and forest mensuration. In addition, in co-operation with Dr. J. F. Heard, Director of the Dunlap Observatory, a stand arboretum of native and exotic tree species is being established on the grounds of the Observatory at Richmond Hill, each species being represented in a block 1/10 of an acre in area.

[4]In August 1960, the Department of Forestry was established by the Dominion Government and incorporates the Forestry Branch, the Forest Products Laboratories, and the Division of Forest Biology.

IX. Undergraduate and Alumni Affairs

DESPITE CONSTANT CHANGE in the membership of the student body, university undergraduates invariably organize themselves in groups and teams in order to share their interests and participate in various kinds of extra-curricular activity. Forestry undergraduates are no exception, and a history of the Faculty would not be complete without some account of these activities, which may be grouped as social, literary, and athletic. No one who has participated wholeheartedly in one or another of the major student undertakings can doubt their value in developing good fellowship and *esprit de corps*, in broadening one's university experience, and indeed in contributing to one's general education.

THE FORESTERS' CLUB

From the beginning the extra-curricular programme of the Faculty has been centred in the Foresters' Club, which was formed by the undergraduates in November 1908, J. H. White being the first president. The Club developed rapidly until the First World War, when in common with many other student organizations it lapsed for a period, to be reorganized in October 1919, at a meeting of the students under the chairmanship of A. W. Bentley. Since that time it has been continuously active and has made a considerable and generally constructive contribution to the life of the Faculty.

From the beginning, the main purpose of the Club has been to provide an open forum for discussion and the opportunity for students to meet with and hear from the leaders of the wood-using industries, the forestry profession, and allied fields of science. From the minutes of the Club, it appears that this purpose has been well served over the years. Also, from time to time the students themselves have taken part in debates and other forms of public speaking, and from the accounts of the meetings this type of activity has been consistently the most successful. Interest in debating has increased recently, perhaps as a result of the Alumni Association presenting a challenge cup for competition among the different years.

The Club provides committees to organize the annual social functions in which staff and students participate; it has prepared and distributed two editions of a mimeographed pamphlet entitled *Silvicultural Characteristics of Canadian Trees*, the first edition of which appeared in 1914;[1] it maintains liaison with university student groups and promotes special events such as the entries in float parades and campaigning for blood donors; it provides the opportunity to discuss matters of Faculty and University interest; nearly every graduate will recall discussion at one time or another on such matters as the Forestry yell, the design of a Faculty crest, the installation of a telephone in the Forestry building for student use, the distribution of tickets for the Hart House masquerade and Sunday evening concerts, and, in a more serious vein, the opportunities for student employment or the defects and deficiencies of the curriculum. Incidentally, participation of the Faculty in University events has generally been maintained at a high level, as for example the forestry entries in the Homecoming Float Parade which won first prize in 1948 and 1957, and have received Honourable Mention on a number of other occasions.

For a time the Club was responsible through committees for the athletic and literary programme of the students. However, in 1921 a separate Athletic Association was formed, and in 1948 the publication of the annual magazine (see p. 86) was placed under a separate editorial board; the officers of these organizations as well as of the Club itself are elected annually.

Many graduates will have pleasant memories of "Stunt Nite," though the event and circumstances this name brings to mind will vary a good deal, depending on the period when the individual attended the University. "Stunt Nite" is rather indefinite in origin, but began about 1911, and for the first few years was truly forestry in character and certainly different from the usual run of university entertainment. On these occasions staff and students, dressed in bush clothes, gathered about the campfire in an open area near the old forestry building in Queen's Park. There they recounted their experiences in the field and gave talks and demonstrations on various aspects of camping and wood craft, including such practical activities as camp cooking, portaging,

[1]A second edition was issued in 1948 and a revision entitled *Seed Characteristics of Canadian Trees* in 1952.

and the handling of pack ponies. The key character for this last event was "Booze" (or on occasion referred to as "Bottle"), a model pack-horse, if ever there was one, the creation of the late R. G. Lewis, '12. This programme ended with a meal prepared over the fire by the two students who had the honour of being elected first and second cooks for the occasion. Usually these activities were sufficient to attract the girls from nearby Queen's Hall, and often the "Stunt Nite" of this period concluded with an impromptu dance in the common room; by 1913 Queen's Hall had become definitely involved in the preparations for "Stunt Nite," particularly in the culinary department.

The same pattern of outdoor activity was followed for a brief period after the First World War, but no doubt influenced by the sophistication of the post-war era, the foresters, though still wearing bush clothes, had moved into the brightly decorated library of the school to dance with their invited guests and eat food prepared and served by the freshmen. Concurrently, a "smoker" had been inaugurated, at which skits on various topical events were presented by the students of each of the different years. After a time the "smoker" disappeared, but the skit idea was incorporated in "Stunt Nite," and by the early thirties became a requirement for the first-year students alone to perform. Gone were the days of "Booze," flapjacks, and the diamond hitch. "Stunt Nite" now moved into Hart House, and, although bush clothes were still in order, supper was served in the Great Hall, entertainment was provided by students and sometimes members of staff, and dancing took place in the East Common Room to the strains of one of the local orchestras. Soon the student entertainment was supplemented by outside talent and then abandoned entirely, as according to the records it was felt that stunts and skits "took up time that could be spent more profitably in other ways."

"Stunt Nite" now moved from Hart House to downtown Toronto, and although for a few years plaid shirts and a camping scene in one corner of the dance floor retained something of a forestry atmosphere, the evolution was soon complete, and "Stunt Nite" became simply an undergraduate dance, known in recent years as the Fall Frolic or Woodchoppers' Ball.

In the meantime, the typically forestry aspects of undergraduate entertainment have been transferred to the Winter Carnival, or that portion of it which is held on the Caledon Hills Farm. There, the students of the Faculty have taken the lead in promoting competition in such activities as "orienteering," log bucking, and overnight camping. Caledon Hills Farm is also the site nowadays for freshman initiation, the main project being a tree-planting bee with the freshmen doing the planting.

The annual banquet has been and still is the principal social event of the year, though it too has changed with the changing fashions and with the growing influence of the distaff side, since it was first held in 1912. Then and for some years thereafter, it was a formal affair for students, staff, and their male guests only. Following dinner, often in the Great Hall, the party adjourned to the Music Room for a congenial evening of discussion and to hear the speeches of guests invited for the occasion. That little time would have been available for lighter entertainment on these occasions will be apparent from the toast list for the second annual banquet held in McConkey's restaurant on January 30, 1913.

The King	Dr. C. D. Howe
The University	President Falconer
The Faculty	Dr. B. E. Fernow
The Dominion Forest Service	R. H. Campbell
Railway Forestry	R. D. Prettie
Conservation	Clyde Leavitt
Forestry in Ontario	E. J. Zavitz
Forestry in Quebec	G. C. Piche
Private Forestry in Canada	Ellwood Wilson

In more recent years, the banquet has taken the form of a dinner-dance under the aegis of the Athletic Association, at which colours and trophies are awarded to students who have been outstanding in sports during the past year.

A spring dance or At Home, which was held for a number of years in the Music Room of Hart House and attended by members of the Club, graduates, and representatives of various faculty organizations, has been discontinued for the past few years.

An event that was never in danger of coming under feminine influence took place for a number of years in the Hart House pool in the form of a primitive and vigorous game of water polo played between the freshmen (without option) and the rest of the undergraduates.

THE *NEWS LETTER* AND *ANNUAL RING*

Almost from the beginning, the students of the Faculty have shown an interest in establishing contact with the graduates through some form of publication. The first "news release" from the Foresters' Club was prepared by Allan Mulloy, '18, in 1917, mainly for and about graduates and undergraduates who were serving with the armed forces. A similar report was prepared in the following year. No doubt both of these were of much interest to Alumni in bringing together news of each other's activities and of forestry developments at home.

In 1921 a letter was sent to all graduates, informing them of activities in the Faculty; as a result of a suggestion made at that time, a directory of graduates was prepared and distributed in 1922 and 1923.

At a meeting of the Foresters' Club in November 1923, it was suggested that a magazine be prepared for distribution to the Alumni. This was approved and in the spring of 1924 the first Club Annual or News Letter was issued; subsequently this appeared annually in mimeographed form until 1936, and biennially thereafter until 1946. These bulletins, which were distributed to all the Alumni, gave the highlights of student activities, news items of graduates, articles from members of staff and Alumni, and, in some issues, continued the directory of names and addresses of graduates and past students.

The aim of these bulletins, as stated in the preface of the first edition, was to produce a magazine type of publication. However, it was not possible to do this until after the Second Word War, when, with many more students to share the work and provide greater financial resources, the *Annual Ring* was brought into being. This publication has appeared annually over the past thirteen years and has been maintained at a high standard throughout.

THE ATHLETIC ASSOCIATION

The Faculty has always been active and well represented in athletics. While a few students have been outstanding in senior intercollegiate competition, the main interest has been centred on the intramural programme of the University, and in many years the Faculty has had the highest proportional representation of any group on the campus. While the students have always given a good account of themselves, and many sectional championships have been won, the outstanding achievement is, of course, to win an intramural championship. Up to 1952, there was only one over-all competition for these championships, and in this period the foresters were successful in winning the Sifton Cup for basketball in 1930, the Mulock Cup for football in 1950, and the Reed Trophy, emblematic of the over-all intramural championship for the University, in 1951. Since the establishment of two divisions of competition, forestry teams have won the second division in basketball in 1953, hockey in 1953, volleyball in 1953, 1954, and 1955, and soccer in 1956, 1958, and 1959.

That not all forestry teams have been outstanding successes will be apparent from the following comment in a newsletter referring to the hockey team of that year: "The forwards were very fast—indeed, when they really got going, you could almost see them moving. Just like last year, the only goal the forwards scored was scored by a defenseman. That sure must be a record!"

With small enrolment, the financing of equipment for athletic events has always been a major problem. Thus in 1914, it required motions at two meetings of the Foresters' Club to ensure that one of the members be reimbursed for the purchase of a football. Similar problems have arisen from time to time, but have become less serious in recent years as financial support has been given the Athletic Association by members of the Alumni. Occasionally, because of small numbers and with the object of fielding a competitive rugby team, forestry students have joined with those from other faculties, but so far this has not proved particularly successful.

THE ALUMNI

A professional faculty can be greatly strengthened in its work if it has the support of interested and active Alumni, who should understand better than any other group the objectives it is striving for and the problems involved. In Alumni affairs, the Faculty of Forestry has been well served.

Prior to 1927, the Forestry Alumni, though not organized on a formal basis, had joined together as a group to undertake one or two projects, including the placing of a bronze plaque in the Forestry Building in 1926 in memory of the Alumni who had been killed in the First World War.

In 1927, at the suggestion of Dr. J. H. White, a poll was taken among the graduates of the Faculty to determine their interest in forming an Alumni association. The result of this poll as reported in the *News Letter* was favourable, though by no means unanimous, and in January 1928, a meeting of the Alumni was held under the chairmanship of Dr. White. At this meeting the Forestry Alumni Association was formed, officers elected, and a constitution adopted. This constitution was published in the *News Letter* of that year, and in it the objects of the Association are stated as follows: "(a) to organize the Alumni of the Faculty of Forestry of the University of Toronto for the purpose of advancing the interests and promoting the welfare of the Faculty and its Alumni, and (b) to acquire membership in the Alumni Federation of the University of Toronto for the purposes of the objects of the said Federation." In the same *News Letter* it was pointed out that "The Forestry Alumni Association is one medium through which the graduate forester can not only keep in touch with what his fellow graduate is doing but with the Faculty of Forestry itself."

During the first few years after its formation, the Forestry Alumni Association worked closely with the Faculty in such undertakings as the revision of the curriculum and the publication of the *News Letter*. However, during the greater part of that period represented by the economic depression and the Second World War the Association was largely inactive, and it was not until 1948 that steps were taken to reorganize it with a view to developing an effective auxiliary in the work of the Faculty. In the fall of 1949 at the time of the forty-first annual meeting of the Canadian Society of Forest Engineers, about one hundred members of the Alumni gathered together for dinner in the Great Hall, Hart House, to meet with officers of the University and the University Alumni Association, and discuss afresh the purpose and objectives of Alumni participation in University and Faculty affairs. At this time also a feature article on the Faculty of Forestry by K. G. Fensom, '24, appeared in the *Varsity Graduate* (16).

While membership has never been large, the Association has made a substantial contribution to the work of the Faculty over the past ten years, particularly in the initiation and support of the following undertakings:

(i) two first-year admission scholarships of the value of $300 and $250 annually,

(ii) the Grace McAree Memorial Fund ($1,000) for the purchase of books and other publications for the library,

(iii) a bronze plaque in the Forestry Building to the memory of those Alumni who were killed in the Second World War,

(iv) annual financial assistance to the Athletic Association of the Faculty for the purchase of sports equipment,

(v) encouragement of debating among the undergraduates and the donation of a challenge cup for competition among the different years,

(vi) assistance towards the publication of this account of the Faculty history.

For the Alumni as a whole, it is gratifying to record, in connection with the National Fund (1959–60), that of all the constituents of the University, Forestry (under the chairmanship of G. W. Phipps, '26) had the highest over-all gift average ($309).

WAR SERVICE

Mention has been made in earlier chapters of the many graduates and students of this Faculty who served in the armed services of their country in two world wars. Of these men, 15 gave their lives in the war of 1914–18 and 5 in the war of 1939–45. Their names are set down below as inscribed on the two bronze tablets that have been placed in their memory in the Forestry Building by the Alumni.

Members of the Faculty of Forestry who were killed in action during the war of 1914–18:

James D. Aiken
Charles L. Anderson
George E. Bothwell
George G. Bricker
Robert A. R. Campbell
James R. Chamberlain
Albert E. Cuzner

Kenneth B. Downie
Harold E. Edmonds
Alister M. Mackenzie
Ronald M. Richards
Frank B. Robertson
Frederic G. Stupart
Arnold M. Thurston

John A. Trebilcock

Members of the Faculty of Forestry who were killed in action during the war of 1939–45:

Francis A. BrodribbJames H. Cooper
Reginald J. L. FowlerRobert Heggie
Robert H. Wilson

FROM GENERATION TO GENERATION

In this account of undergraduate and Alumni affairs, it is of significance to record a continuity of interest from one generation to another in forestry as a career; this is apparent in the number of second generation foresters who have enrolled in the Faculty in recent years, sons of fathers who had taken forestry at Toronto or at another forestry school. The following list of those representing two generations in the profession of forestry has been brought up to date to include students enrolled in the Faculty at the present time (1960).

First generation	*Second generation*
P. Addison, '29, Regional Forester, Department of Lands and Forests	W. D. Addison, '63, Forestry student, U. of T.
L. R. Andrews, '13 (retired)	J. R. T. Andrews, '48, Forester, Hunting Survey Corpn. Ltd., Toronto
B. F. Avery, Yale, '14, President, Canadian Forestry Assn., Espanola	D. D. Avery, '46, The KVP Company Ltd., Espanola
G. W. Bayly, '13 (died 1941)	G. H. Bayly, '39, Assistant Deputy Minister, Department of Lands and Forests, Toronto
J. A. Brodie, '23, Chief, Timber Branch, Department of Lands and Forests, Toronto	J. D. Brodie, 61, Forestry student, U. of T.
A. F. Buell, '31, Vice-President in charge of Woodlands, The E. B. Eddy Co. Ltd., Hull, P.Q.	T. A. Buell, '56, Camp Foreman, Kimberly-Clark Pulp and Paper Co. Ltd., Longlac
R. S. Carman, '21 (retired)	R. D. Carman, '54, Forester, Timber Branch, Department of Lands and Forests, Toronto
C. H. Irwin, '22, Sherwood Forest Camp, Carnarvon	J. D. Irwin, '51, Forest Products Laboratories of Canada, Ottawa
J. W. McNutt, '32, President, William Milne & Sons Ltd., North Bay	J. F. K. McNutt, '61, Forestry student, U. of T.
M. B. Morison, U.N.B., '24, Assistant Chief, Timber Branch, Department of Lands and Forests, Toronto	R. W. Morison, '54, Forester, Kimberly-Clark Pulp and Paper Co. Ltd., Longlac

UNDERGRADUATE AND ALUMNI AFFAIRS 93

H. H. Parsons, '25, Consulting Forester, Toronto

W. D. Start, '30, Manager of Forest Research, Inventories and Planning, The Ontario-Minnesota Pulp and Paper Company, Limited, Kenora

J. V. Stewart, '24 (died 1931)

J. F. Turnbull, '22 (retired)

W. E. Willson, '25, Assistant to Manager of Woodlands, Abitibi Power & Paper Co. Ltd., Toronto

C. C. Wright, U.N.B., '31, Superintendent, Industrial Relations, Woodlands, Spruce Falls Power and Paper Co. Ltd., Kapuskasing

M. J. Morison, '59, Forester, Kenora District, Department of Lands and Forests

D. G. Parsons, '54, Forester, Johns Manville Co., North Bay

E. H. Start, '63, Forestry student, U. of T.

J. V. Stewart, U.N.B., '55, Graduate student in Forestry, U. of T.

N. J. Turnbull, '49, District Superintendent, Spruce Falls Power and Paper Co. Ltd., Kapuskasing

J. L. Willson, '64, Forestry student, U. of T.

D. R. Wright, '62, Forestry student, U. of T.

Appendix I

UNIVERSITY OF TORONTO

Statute Number 491
Regarding the establishment of a School of Forestry in the
University of Toronto and the curriculum therefor
Passed January 9th, 1903

By the Senate of the University of Toronto,
Be it enacted:
1. The School of Forestry is hereby established in the University of Toronto.
2. The following shall be the curriculum leading to a Diploma in Forestry:
3. Entrance: Candidates for a Diploma must have passed in the subjects of Junior Matriculation, omitting Latin; or be of the . . . .
4. The course shall extend over three winter and two summer sessions.
5. The subjects of instruction and examination shall be as follows:

First Year: Elementary Biology with Laboratory work; Elementary Chemistry with Laboratory work; Elementary Physics; Elementary Geology; English and Mathematics of the First Year General Course in Arts; Scientific French and German.

Second Year: Morphology and Physiology of Phanerogamic Plants; Forest Botany; Forest Zoology; Geology and Mineralogy with the origin and nature of soils; General principles of Forestry including Forest Physiography; Meteorology; Sylviculture; Practical Physics; Surveying and Drawing; and Forest Measurements.

The Summer Session of the Second Year shall be devoted to practical work in the Forest in illustration of the foregoing subjects.

Third Year: Cryptogamic Botany, Diseases of Trees due (1) to physical conditions, (2) to attacks of plants and animals; Physical characteristics and commercial utilization of the various kinds of woods; Forestry, including the administration and protection of Forests, Lumbering, Construction of Forest Roads, Administration of the Forest Resources of Ontario, Provincial Forest Laws and Regulations.

The Summer Session of the Third Year shall be devoted to practical work in the Forest in illustration of the foregoing subjects.

[seal]   VICE-CHANCELLOR

Countersigned
JAMES BREBNER, Registrar

Appendix II

THE ENROLMENT OF STUDENTS IN THE FACULTY OF FORESTRY 1907–61
(Grouped in ten-year periods)

Year	Graduate students[a]	Undergraduate students							Special and occasional students	Total enrolment	No. of grads.
		First year	Second year	Third year	Fourth year	Fifth[b] year	Sixth[b] year	Total			
1907–8	—	3	1	2	—	—	—	6	—	6	—
1908–9	—	15	3	3	2	—	—	23	—	23	1
1909–10	—	15	15	5	3	—	—	38	1	39	2
1910–11	—	9	11	13	7	—	—	40	5	45	4
1911–12	—	7	5	15	12	1	—	40	—	40	9
1912–13	—	13	10	6	12	—	—	41	4	45	11
1913–14	—	18	10	7	9	1	1	46	1	47	7
1914–15	—	16	8	11	8	1	—	44	—	44	7
1915–16	—	1	14	6	10	1	—	32	—	32	9
1916–17	—	3	—	2	5	—	—	10	—	10	3
TOTALS, 1907–17	—	100[c]							11		53
1917–18	1	4	1	—	4	—	—	9	—	10	2
1918–19	—	6	3	1	5	—	—	15	—	15	3
1919–20	—	20	15	7	2	1	1	46	2	48	3
1920–21	—	20	17	10	6	—	—	53	2	55	6
1921–22	—	21	13	11	13	—	—	58	4	62	11
1922–23	—	10	14	13	12	—	—	49	—	49	10
1923–24	—	6	10	13	13	—	—	42	—	42	14
1924–25	1	12	6	12	12	—	—	42	—	43	10
1925–26	1	13	11	7	13	—	—	44	—	45	13
1926–27	2	21	10	10	9	—	—	50	—	52	9
TOTALS, 1917–27	5	133							8		81

[a]Candidates for both the M.Sc.F. and F.E. degrees. For the M.Sc.F. degree the candidate may be required to register for two years. Hence there will be some duplication in these figures.
[b]These are the last two years of a combined course, which made it possible to qualify for both B.Sc.F. and B.A. degrees and was offered from 1910 to 1921.
[c]Approximately 5 per cent of this and similar totals below represents students who repeat first year.

APPENDIX II—*continued*

Year	Graduate students[a]	Undergraduate students							Special and occasional students	Total enrol-ment	No. of grads.
		First year	Second year	Third year	Fourth year	Fifth[b] year	Sixth[b] year	Total			
1927–28	1	24	15	9	10	—	—	58	—	59	10
1928–29	1	22	22	12	10	—	—	66	—	67	9
1929–30	—	16	16	19	11	—	—	62	—	62	11
1930–31	—	17	13	13	18	—	—	61	—	61	18
1931–32	1	28	17	10	13	—	—	68	1	70	13
1932–33	5	23	24	13	8	—	—	68	—	73	8
1933–34	4	9	16	22	12	—	—	59	—	63	11
1934–35	1	7	10	13	22	—	—	52	—	53	21
1935–36	2	13	7	8	14	—	—	42	—	44	14
1936–37	—	21	9	6	7	—	—	43	—	43	9
TOTALS, 1927–37	15	180							1		124
1937–38	—	8	12	5	6	—	—	31	—	31	6
1938–39	1	14	4	9	6	—	—	33	—	34	4
1939–40	—	19	13	2	7	—	—	41	—	41	7
1940–41	1	18	16	16	3	—	—	53	1	55	3
1941–42	—	13	7	12	10	—	—	42	2	44	10
1942–43	—	15	4	5	7	—	—	31	3	34	9
1943–44	1	18	15	4	2	—	—	39	5	45	1
1944–45	2	28	17	13	3	—	—	61	6	69	5
1945–46	2	104	42	19	12	—	—	177	—	179	13
1946–47	4	107	91	37	22	—	—	257	—	261	22
TOTALS, 1937–47	11	344							17		80

APPENDIX II—continued

Year	Graduate students[a]	Undergraduate students							Special and occasional students	Total enrolment	No. of grads.
		First year	Second year	Third year	Fourth year	Fifth[b] year	Sixth[b] year	Total			
1947–48	3	61	98	87	36	—	—	282	4	289	36
1948–49	3	56	66	93	87	—	—	302	—	305	86
1949–50	2	38	54	64	89	—	—	245	—	247	90
1950–51	7	49	34	46	62	—	—	191	—	198	56
1951–52	8	44	39	27	44	—	—	154	—	162	46
1952–53	2	33	38	39	23	—	—	133	—	135	23
1953–54	4	34	29	28	37	—	—	128	—	132	37
1954–55	2	24	33	25	24	—	—	106	—	108	19
1955–56	2	10	25	28	23	—	—	86	—	88	21
1956–57	6	19	12	23	25	—	—	79	—	85	25
TOTALS, 1947–57	39	368							4		439
1957–58	4	21	16	15	21	—	—	73	—	77	21
1958–59	9	26	18	18	12	—	—	74	—	83	12
1959–60	6	27	21	21	14	—	—	84	4	94	13
1960–61	9	39	23	21	15	—	—	98	—	107	17
TOTALS, 1957–61	28	113							4		63
GRAND TOTALS	98[d]	1238							45		840

[d] A total of 36 F.E., M.A. (in Forestry) and M.Sc.F. have been granted during this period. A number of those registered did not complete the requirements, and some of those recorded in the earlier years (viz. 1931–35) may have taken their work in the Departments of Botany or of Zoology. Of the 24 registered as graduate students in the last three years (1958–61), three have completed the requirements for their degree and all but one of the remainder are expected to do so within the next two years.

Appendix III

OFFICERS OF UNDERGRADUATE AND GRADUATE ORGANIZATIONS

The following are the names of those elected President of the Foresters' Club and Athletic Association and those appointed as permanent secretaries of each of the graduating classes.

PRESIDENTS OF THE FORESTERS' CLUB		PERMANENT SECRETARIES OF GRADUATING CLASSES	
Year	Name	Year	Name
1908–9	J. H. White	1909	J. H. White
1909–10	T. W. Dwight	1910	T. W. Dwight
1910–11	D. R. Cameron	1911	D. R. Cameron
1911–12	E. H. Finlayson	1912	E. H. Finlayson
1912–13	H. R. Christie	1913	H. R. Christie
1913–14	F. B. Robertson	1914	R. L. Campbell
1914–15	C. H. Morse	1915	W. A. Delahey
1915–16	J. D. Aiken	1916	P. McEwen
1916–17	G. A. Mulloy	1917	R. A. N. Johnston
1917–18	G. A. Mulloy	1918	G. A. Mulloy
1918–19		1919	W. M. Robertson
1919–20	A. W. Bentley	1920	W. G. Wright
1920–21	H. M. Hughson	1921	A. W. Bentley
1921–22	J. L. Van Camp	1922	M. J. Commins
1922–23	W. D. Cram	1923	E. Druce
1923–24	J. D. B. MacFarlane	1924	R. C. Hosie
1924–25	W. B. Greenwood	1925	H. H. Parsons
1925–26	G. R. Lane	1926	G. R. Lane
1926–27	W. E. Gimby	1927	H. L. McCausland
1927–28	J. W. Johnson	1928	M. A. Adamson
1928–29	C. H. Bastock	1929	A. P. Leslie
1929–30	G. S. Andrews	1930	G. R. Sonley
1930–31	L. E. Simpson	1931	J. S. Walker
1931–32	J. W. McNutt	1932	H. W. Beall
1932–33	R. S. Young	1933	R. E. Sewell
1933–34	A. L. K. Switzer	1934	A. L. K. Switzer
1934–35	D. I. Crossley	1935	W. H. Bennett
1935–36	V. H. Phelps	1936	J. L. Farrar
1936–37	T. R. Powell	1937	J. H. Cooper
1937–38	F. S. Hick	1938	E. R. Sexsmith
1938–39	W. R. Grinnell	1939	G. H. Bayly
1939–40	H. N. Middleton	1940	S. Y. Yavner
1940–41	C. G. Hadley	1941	C. G. Hadley
1941–42	J. H. Hope	1942	
1942–43	J. S. McBride	1943	H. T. Renaud
1943–44	W. R. McKay	1944	
1944–45	J. R. F. Blais	1945	K. B. Turner
1945–46	D. Naysmith	1946	R. Schafer
1946–47	G. L. Puttock	1947	G. L. Puttock

Year	Name	Year	Name
1947–48	J. W. Giles	1948	L. S. Hamilton
1948–49	D. H. Burton	1949	J. E. C. Pringle
1949–50	E. K. E. Dreyer	1950	D. C. Mason
1950–51	S. B. K. Brackenbury	1951	J. L. Mullen
1951–52	C. W. Gregory	1952	J. D. Coats
1952–53	D. T. Bell	1953	O. L. Loucks
1953–54	H. G. Hooke	1954	R. J. Burgar
1954–55	W. K. Fullerton	1955	G. F. Weetman
1955–56	J. I. Johnston	1956	D. A. W. Richards
1956–57	J. R. McMullen	1957	D. C. F. Fayle
1957–58	W. D. Tieman	1958	W. A. G. Hannaford
1958–59	M. J. Morison	1959	
1959–60	K. H. Reese	1960	E. G. Osler
1960–61	E. B. MacDougall		

PRESIDENTS OF THE ATHLETIC ASSOCIATION

Undergraduate athletics were administered through a committee of the Foresters' Club until 1921 when the Athletic Association was formed.

Year	Name	Year	Name
1921–22	W. A. E. Pepler	1941–42	R. E. Mullin
1922–23	J. V. Stewart	1942–43	A. F. Allman
1923–24	A. R. Fenwick	1943–44	M. R. MacKay
1924–25	G. W. Phipps	1944–45	H. D. Graham
1925–26	T. H. Ryan	1945–46	M. P. Lawson
1926–27	D. McK. Parker	1946–47	C. J. H. Campbell
1927–28	L. Simpson	1947–48	W. M. Bastedo
1928–29	F. N. Wiley	1948–49	W. G. McKeon
1929–30	F. L. Flatt	1949–50	A. C. Poole
1930–31	F. L. Flatt	1950–51	W. C. Dowsett
1931–32	D. W. Christie	1951–52	R. A. McPhail
1932–33	R. D. K. Acheson	1952–53	W. E. Earle
1933–34	F. L. Stevens	1953–54	R. J. Burgar
1934–35	G. Millson	1954–55	A. E. Moyer
1935–36	D. M. Dyer	1955–56	R. G. Armstrong
1936–37	D. P. Cowan	1956–57	J. A. Guertin
1937–38	J. Barron	1957–58	W. B. Newman
1938–39	G. H. Bayly	1958–59	E. G. Wilson
1939–40	J. E. Reynolds	1959–60	R. J. Carrow
1940–41	S. N. Ballantyne	1960–61	K. P. Campbell

EDITORIAL CHAIRMEN FOR PUBLICATIONS OF THE FORESTERS' CLUB

Year	Title or Form	Editor or Chairman of Editorial Committee
1917	a news letter	G. A. Mulloy
1918	a news letter	—
—	—	—
1921	a news letter	E. Druce
—	—	—
1924	Club Annual	—
1925	” ”	—

APPENDIX III 101

Year	Title or Form	Editor or Chairman of Editorial Committee
1926	News Letter	A. W. Goodfellow
1927	Annual News Letter	W. E. Steele
1928	" " "	L. R. Seheult
1929	" " "	C. W. R. Day
1930	" " "	A. S. L. Barnes
1931	" " "	J. S. Walker
1932	" " "	J. W. McNutt
1933	" " "	R. E. Sewell
1934	Foresters' Club Annual News Letter	R. I. Young
1935	" " "	K. M. Mayall
1936	" " "	J. L. Farrar
—	—	—
1940	News Letter	Q. F. Hess
—	—	—
1942	" "	
1944	Foresters' Club News Letter	M. R. McKay
1946	" " " "	K. W. Hearnden
1948	The Annual Ring	J. D. Osborne
1949	" " "	R. A. Smith
1950	" " "	J. R. M. Williams
1951	" " "	A. S. Morris
1952	" " "	K. W. Horton
1953	" " "	O. L. Loucks
1954	" " "	G. Pierpoint
1955	" " "	G. Pierpoint
1956	" " "	D. A. W. Richards
1957	" " "	D. C. F. Fayle
1958	" " "	W. A. G. Hannaford
1959	" " "	E. B. MacDougall
1960	" " "	E. B. MacDougall
1961	" " "	L. S. McCoy

OFFICERS OF THE FORESTRY ALUMNI ASSOCIATION SINCE 1948

	President	Secretary-Treasurer
July 1948–July 1949	F. S. Newman	J. F. Sharpe
July 1949–July 1951	G. W. Phipps	L. S. Hamilton (Secretary) G. H. Sonley (Treasurer)
July 1951–July 1953	G. H. Sonley	C. R. Groves
July 1953–July 1955	J. B. Matthews	A. D. Hall
July 1955–July 1957	E. Bonner	E. L. Hughes
July 1957–July 1959	W. A. Delahey	H. N. Middleton
July 1959–July 1961	A. L. Bray	E. F. Ault

Appendix IV

ORIGINAL CURRICULUM, FACULTY OF FORESTRY, UNIVERSITY OF TORONTO, 1907

I Year

Mathematics: (a) Algebra, Plane Trigonometry, Analytical Geometry, (b) Calculus (optional).
Physics: Elementary Mechanics, Hydrostatics, Heat.
Chemistry: Elementary Chemistry.
Biology: (a) Elementary Biology, (b) Elementary Zoology, (c) Elementary Botany, (d) Descriptive Dendrology.
Forestry: Synoptical Course.
German
French
Summer Work: Botanical Collection.

II Year

Chemistry: Elementary Organic Chemistry.
Biology: (a) Phanerogamic Botany, (b) Vegetable Physiology and Ecology (Biological Dendrology).
Geology: (a) Elementary Mineralogy, (b) Petrography, (c) Elementary Geology, (d) Origin and Physics of Soil.
Surveying and Map Drawing
Forest Geography
Summer Work: employment on Forest Survey and Field Zoology.

III Year

Chemistry: Physical Chemistry.
Geology: (a) Stratigraphical Geology and Physiography, (b) Meteorology and Climatology.
Biology: (a) Cryptogamic Botany, (b) Diseases of Trees, (c) Economic Entomology.
Surveying, Topographical
Forestry: (a) Mensuration, (b) Silviculture, (c) Forest Utilization, (d) Forest Protection.

IV Year

Mathematics: Actuarial Science.
Chemistry: (a) Applied Chemistry, (b) Biochemistry of Plants (optional).
Political Economy
Canadian Constitutional History
Forestry: (a) Management and Working Plans, (b) Valuation and Finance, (c) History of Forestry, (d) Administration, (e) Seminary in German Silvicultural Literature, (f) Timber Physics and Wood Technology.

Appendix V

UNDERGRADUATE SCHOLARSHIPS, PRIZES, AND MEDALS, FACULTY OF FORESTRY, UNIVERSITY OF TORONTO, 1960

Award	Donors	Terms of Award
Forestry Memorial Scholarships (two)	Anonymous donor (1942) and University of Toronto Forestry Alumni Association	Primarily the standing obtained at the Ontario Grade XIII examination, candidates being required to have an average of at least 66 per cent.
John Lewis Foster Scholarship	Messrs. K. H., C. W., and C. B. Foster	Primarily on the standing obtained at the Ontario Grade XIII examination, candidates being required to have attended for at least two years in a secondary school in one of the counties of Hastings, Peterborough, Frontenac, or Lennox-Addington.
The White Pine Bureau Scholarship	Canadian Lumbermen's Association	Highest standing with honours at the annual examinations of first year.
The F. K. Morrow Forestry Scholarship	The late Frederick Keenan Morrow, Esq., O.B.E.	Highest standing with honours at the annual examinations of the third year.
The Spruce Falls Power and Paper Company, Limited, Scholarships (four)	The Spruce Falls Power and Paper Company, Limited	Four scholarships to be awarded to students in the second and third years, two in each year to the students obtaining the highest average in selected subjects in (a) the biological field, and (b) the mathematical field, in each case the student being required to have obtained honours in the final examinations of the year.
The Goodman Scholarship	Mr. O. S. Goodman	Highest standing in Silviculture, the student having obtained honours in the final examinations of the third year.

The Osmose Wood Preserving Scholarship	The Osmose Wood Preserving Company of Canada Limited	The student obtaining the highest average in the subjects: Wood Structure and Technology, Forest Utilization, and Cellulose Industries.
P. D. Leslie Scholarship	Mr. A. P. Leslie	Highest standing in the fourth year Forest Management Project.
R. P. Wright Memorial Scholarship	Mrs. R. P. Wright	Highest standing in Wood Technology, the candidate having obtained honours in the final examination of third year.
The Harold S. Edmonds Prize	Miss Dorothea M. Edmonds and Mr. C. W. Edmonds	Highest standing with honours at the annual examinations of the second year.
Canadian Institute of Forestry Medal	The Canadian Institute of Forestry	The fourth year student who in the opinion of the Committee of Award has been outstanding in his class, taking into consideration academic qualification and participation in Faculty activities.
Schlich Memorial Fund Award	Schlich Memorial Fund (held in trust by the Canadian Institute of Forestry)	The student who has the highest average in Silviculture for both the third and fourth year examinations.

Appendix VI

MEMBERS OF THE STAFF, FACULTY OF FORESTRY, UNIVERSITY OF TORONTO 1907–60

TEACHING STAFF

B. E. Fernow, LL.D., 1907–19
A. H. D. Ross, M.A., M.F., 1907–14
E. J. Zavitz, B.A., M.S.F. (part-time) 1907–8
C. D. Howe, M.A., Ph.D., 1908–41
J. H. White, M.A., B.Sc.F., Ph.D., 1907–46
W. N. Millar, B.Sc., M.F., 1914–33
T. W. Dwight, B.Sc.F., M.F., 1922–57
R. C. Hosie, B.Sc.F., M.A., 1924–
G. G. Cosens, B.Sc.F., M.A., 1934–47
J. W. B. Sisam, B.Sc.F., M.F., D.Sc., 1945–

A. S. Michell, C.D., B.Sc.F., M.F., 1946–
D. V. Love, B.Sc.F., M.F., 1946–
F. G. Jackson, B.Sc.F., 1946–52
J. A. C. Grant, B.Sc.F., 1947–55
A. D. Hall, B.Sc.F., 1949–
G. A. Hills, M.Sc.A. (part-time), 1951–5
K. A. Armson, B.Sc.F., Dip. For., 1952–
J. L. Farrar, B.Sc.F., M.F., Ph.D., 1956–
N. L. Kissick, B.Sc.F., M.F., 1956–
F. M. Buckingham, B.Sc., M.F., 1957–
E. Jorgensen, M.Sc.F., 1959–

OFFICE STAFF

Miss E. W. Mills, 1912–28
Miss J. I. Fraser, 1928–32
Miss E. G. McAree, 1931–50

Miss M. H. Harman, 1947–
Miss P. M. Balme, B.A., 1950–
Mrs. W. J. McJannet, 1958–

Appendix VII

GRADUATES IN FORESTRY BY YEARS

1909
White, J. H.

1910
Dwight, T. W.
Edgecombe, G. H.

1911
Cameron, D. R.
Ellis, L. M.
Gilmour, J. D.
McDougall, E. G.

1912
Brown, R. M.
Edgar, F. G.
Finlayson, E. H.
Irwin, H. S.
Lewis, R. G.
MacFayden, C.
Manning, E. C.
Scandrett, W. L.
Van Dusen, W. J.

1913
Andrews, L. R.
Bothwell, G. E.
Christie, H. R.
Clark, S. H.
McVickar, F.
Morton, B. R.
Newman, F. S.
Parlow, A. E.
Sadler, S. S.
Tilt, L. C.
Tunstell, G.

1914
Campbell, R. L.
Chamberlin, J. R.
Connell, A. B.
Davison, E. S.
Kynoch, W.
Robertson, F. B.
Smith, G. S.

1915
Delahey, W. A.
Mills, C. R.

Morse, C. H.
Prowd, E. B.
Rance, T. F.
Simmons, J. L.
Sloan, J. M.
Trebilcock, J. A.

1916
Aiken, J. D.
Boyd, W. J.
Dallyn, G. M.
Gilbert, A. V.
Gill, C.B.
Greig, D.
Lyons, R. W.
McEwen, P.
Porteous, H.A.

1917
Johnston, R.A.N.
McCallum, A. W.
Nieuwejaar, O.

1918
Courtnage, R. A.
Mulloy, G. A.

1919
Kay, J.
Linton, G. M.
Robertson, W. M.

1920
Horton, F. H.
Parker, H. A.
Wright, W. G.

1921
Alexander, J. L.
Bentley, A. W.
Carman, R. S.
Clarke, T. A.
Eisler, H. P.
Hughson, H. M.

1922
Doran, A. B.
Irwin, C. H.
Irwin, J. C. W.

McDonald, J. H.
Marritt, I. C.
Pepler, W. A. E.
Sharpe, J. F.
Stewart, K. A.
Thrupp, A. C.
Turnbull, J. F.
Van Camp, J. L.

1923
Brodie, J. A.
Commins, M. J.
Cosens, G. G.
Cram, W. D.
Crosbie, H. W.
Foote, C. E.
Haddow, W. R.
Jenkins, F. T.
MacDougall, F. A.
Westland, C. E.

1924
Ardenne, M.
Brown, J. D.
Burk, A. H.
Druce, E.
Fensom, K. G.
Grant, G. C.
Hosie, R. C.
Kensit, N. M.
Laschinger, E. J.
McKenzie, A. R.
Reid, L. H.
Stewart, J. V.
Walton, J. R.
Whitelaw, W. A.

1925
Archer, C. F.
Batt, C. A.
Bedell, G. H. D.
Fenwick, A. R.
Greenwood, W. B.
Kingston, G. A.
MacFarlane, J. D. B.
Parsons, H. H.
Thomson, G. J.
Willson, W. E.

APPENDIX VII 107

1926
Burrows, T. A.
Goodfellow, A. W.
Halliday, W. E. D.
Krug, H. H.
Lane, G. R.
Macdonald, S. C.
Mackey, T. E.
Munro, D. J.
O'Connor, P. A.
Phipps, G. W.
Ryan, T. H.
Simpson, E. R.
Smith, R. E.

1927
Bayly, G. W.
Connor, L. L.
Gimby, W. E.
Higgins, W. A.
McCausland, H. L.
Putnam, M. M.
Steele, W. E.
Ussher, R. D.
Ward, E. L.

1928
Adamson, M. A.
Goodall, R. F.
Heimburger, C. C.
Johnson, J. W.
McCraw, W. E.
McLaren, D.
Parker, D. M.
Seheult, L. R.
Snow, R. D. L.
Teasdale, J. A.

1929
Addison, P.
Boultbee, R.
Day, C. W. R.
Francis, S. H.
Kelly, T. W.
Leslie, A. P.
Matthews, J. B.
Plahte, F. M.
Robinson, J. M.

1930
Andrews, G. S.
Barnes, A. S. L.
Grainger, E. E.
Gray, D. W.
Leman, A. W.
MacBean, A. P.

Orr, H. V.
Raeburn, J.
Sonley, G. R.
Start, W. D.
Wheatley, A. B.

1931
Bastock, C. H.
Bray, A. S.
Buell, A. F.
Capp, H. E.
Catto, A. T.
Clarke, C. H. D.
Corin, F.
Flatt, F. L.
Goodison, J. C.
Hayward, F. R.
Leslie, F.
Losee, S. T. B.
MacLulich, D. A.
Millar, J. B.
Simpson, L. E.
Walker, J. S.
Walkom, H. C.
Wiley, F. N.

1932
Beall, H. W.
Bennett, W. D.
Bier, J. E.
Choate, G. A.
Christie, D. W. C.
Cooper, C.
Crealock, A.
Eidt, F. E.
Jackson, F. G.
Jackson, J. C.
McNutt, J. W.
Meyer, G. F.
White, L. T.

1933
Acheson, R. D. K.
Ball, G. E.
Brown, A. W. A.
Bullock, R. M.
MacDonald, J. A.
Sewell, R. E.
Townson, J. P.
Young, R. S.

1934
Beatty, W. S.
Bonner, E.
Edwards, W. E.
Howard, C. P.

McEwen, J.
Reeves, E. H.
Stevens, F. L.
Switzer, A. L. K.
Townsend, P. B.
Wilson, M. R.
Young, R. I.

1935
Allen, H. W.
Bennett, W. H.
Breckon, J. L.
Carrique, H. C.
Copland, J. W.
Crossley, D. I.
Faber, W. O.
Garrette, G. G.
Godden, J. H.
Greer, L. F.
Gregson, A. K.
Heggie, R.
Kantola, H. O.
McCrae, C. W. G.
Mayall, K. M.
Millson, G. D.
Mustard, A. J.
Sime, J. R.
Skolko, A. J.
Smith, B. J.
Young, D. R.

1936
Boultbee, F. C.
Carlson, W. S.
Cushing, W. J.
Day, J. C.
Dyer, D. M.
Farrar, J. L.
Golder, S. N.
Harrison, W. C.
Morley, P. M.
Noakes, J. W.
Phelps, V. H.
Porter, A. W.
Stangeby, C. H.
Taylor, M. G.

1937
Bickerstaff, A.
Cooper, J. H.
Cowan, D. P.
Hyslop, R. S.
Larsson, O. G.
Lein, L. M.
Merrett, D. C.

Mundy, G. W.
Powell, T. R.

1938
Barron, J.
Johnstone, H. J.
McConnell, L. E.
Sexsmith, E. R.
Sider, F. E.
Ward, P.

1939
Bayly, G. H.
Hick, F. S.
Murchison, G. H.
Silversides, C. R.

1940
Grinnell, W. R.
Hess, Q. F.
Michell, A. S.
Middleton, H. N.
Reynolds, J. E.
Robb, D. L.
Yavner, S. Y.

1941
Ballantyne, S. N.
Dixon, M. M.
Hadley, C. G.

1942
Bruce, D. S.
Day, B. G.
Eccles, W. R.
Gray, R. H.
Hall, F. L.
Hope, J. H.
Kirk, M. D.
Larsson, H. C.
Mullin, R. E.
Smith, J. O.

1943
Adams, W. W.
Alexander, J. P.
Boissonneau, A. N.
Campbell, D. J.
Davidson, D. L.
McBride, J. S.
Renaud, H. T.
Thurston, W. A. G.

1944
Lee, K. B.

1945
Blais, J. R. F.

Graham, H. D.
Joly de Lotbinière, A.
McKay, M. R.
Turner, K. B.

1946
Avery, D. D.
Chalk, A. W.
Groome, E. S.
Hayes, T. J. F.
Hearnden, K. W.
Hueston, T. W.
Lawson, M. P.
McGee, C. J.
Naysmith, D.
Robinson, J. M.
Schafer, R.
van Vlymen, V. P.
Wyllie, G. W.

1947
Allman, A. F.
Beare, G. E. B.
Boultbee, J. G.
Brown, W. G. E.
Buckley, T. C. E. H.
Campbell, C. J. H.
Carmichael, A. D. J.
Carr, J. A.
Clark, D. C. E.
Cox, G. A.
Foster, W. T.
Fountain, W. C.
Grant, J. A. C.
Halpenny, J. M.
Hambly, R. H.
Jenkins, J. L.
Johnston, W. J.
Kasturik, A. M.
Puttock, G. L.
Robertson, D. C. G.
Shand, R. A.
Taylor, M. D.

1948
Andrews, J. R. T.
Ball, J. S.
Basham, J. T.
Bastedo, W. M.
Beardsell, W. W. J.
Blair, J. H.
Cringan, A. T.
Dance, B. W.
Edwards, R. Y.
Eggertson, E.

Gage, D. E.
Giles, J. W.
Hall, A. D.
Hamilton, L. S.
Hare, P. J.
Hughes, J. R.
Kallio, R. E.
Kissick, N. L.
Linzon, S. N.
Lyon, N. F.
Mennill, J. L.
Moore, W. S.
Morrison, G. R.
Osborne, J. D.
Purdy, A. S.
Robinson, F. C.
Russell, A. A.
Ryan, T. J.
Shand, J. H.
Sinclair, G. A.
Smith, J. T.
Stark, R. W.
Tait, J. E.
Truemner, W. J. D.
Walroth, A. E.
Wilson, G. M.

1949
Atkinson, A. G.
Atkinson, J. M.
Ault, E. F.
Ayer, E. B.
Bagg, E. J. K.
Beckwith, A. F.
Bell, G. W.
Benson, B. B.
Berbee, J. G.
Black, R. L.
Brittain, R. V.
Buchanan, A.
Burton, D. H.
Cameron, G. W.
Christman, D. E.
Connon, P. F. H.
Connor, R. C.
Coyne, G. F.
Cressman, E. M.
Crowhurst, K. G.
Cuff, W. E.
Daly, E. G.
Daubney, P. E.
Donnan, T. C.
Donnelly, J. J.
Dyer, W. G. G.
Eckel, L. H.

APPENDIX VII 109

Edwards, J. G.
Flowers, J. F.
Forfar, R. T.
Forsythe, H. T.
Fraser, J. W.
Fraser, R. C.
Gillespie, E. D.
Griffiths, J. D.
Haig, R. A.
Hall, D. E.
Hamilton, S. R. C.
Herridge, A. J.
Herwig, J. D.
Hilborn, W. H.
Holman, G. E.
Jamieson, J. H.
Johnston, E. F.
Kastrukoff, M.
Lewis, E. A.
Loughlan, R. B.
McElhanney, T. P.
McKeon, W. G.
McMahon, J. M.
McPherson, J. A.
Mascall, D. W. W.
Murphy, K. R. J.
Oliphant, W. L.
Palmer, J. E.
Parks, W. R.
Passmore, R. C.
Peacock, A. H.
Peters, W. D.
Pierce, T. W.
Plouffe, G. T.
Pointing, P. J.
Pollock, P. C.
Pringle, J. E. C.
Ringham, L.
Robinson, F. N.
Royce, C. D.
Ruhl, F. S.
Shaw, D. J.
Shreeve, F. T.
Sloane, N. H.
Smith, B. O.
Smith, R. A.
Smith, V. G.
Somerville, J. T.
Turnbull, N. J.
Turner, A. R.
Vance, D. J.
Walker, J. T.
Warwick, A. J.
Watson, W. C.
Wilde, C. J. R.

Wilkes, G. C.
Wilson, D. R.
Wilson, R. A.
Winter, J. E. F.

1950

Adlam, W. D.
Amos, E. W.
Anderson, E. F.
Anslow, P. E.
Ashenden, G. A.
Bain, G. R.
Balkwill, R. A.
Banks, R. H.
Bartlett, W. A.
Bell, G. C.
Blackwood, C. M.
Booth, L. W.
Bothwell, J. E.
Bunting, W. R.
Burton, C. H.
Cahill, L. G. J.
Cameron, G. M.
Cochrane, A. S.
Cockerill, J.
Connolly, T. W.
Cran, I. M.
Davis, J. T.
Dickenson, J. E.
Digby, W. H.
Dixon, R. M.
Doan, S. A.
Dorland, J. T.
Doull, G. S.
Dreisinger, B. R.
Dreyer, E. K. E.
Fournier, S. A.
Gall, M. E.
Gaughan, J. K.
Genge, G. A.
Ghent, A. W.
Gibson, C. L.
Giles, G. W. R.
Gordon, T. C.
Gourlay, J. F. W.
Greaves, K. D.
Groves, C. R.
Hagar, D. L.
Harvie, P. M. R.
Hawtin, J. A.
Hazell, J. S.
Hughes, E. L.
Hughes, J. D.
Hummel, R. W.
Humphreys, E. R.

Jameson, J. S.
Jarvis, J. M.
Jones, A. R. C.
Julian, R. J.
Kaye, G. V.
Lloyd, T. H.
Lockhart, D. D.
Long, J. F.
Longley, G. M. B.
Lukinuk, S. W.
MacGregor, D. W.
McGinn, W. K.
McKnight, J. R.
Mason, D. C.
Mick, P. A.
Miller, G. H.
Monaghan, J. M.
Openshaw, T. J.
Peacock, D. M.
Penna, D.
Phillips, R. J.
Pochailo, C. J.
Poole, A. C.
Rodwell, R. F.
Scott, D. A.
Sleeman, W. L.
Sleep, V. I.
Stewart, J. C.
Stone, J. D.
Tamosetis, E.
Thomas, H. W. E.
Thomson, R. E.
Usher, J. A.
Wheeler, F. W.
White, D. C.
White, S. B.
Williams, J. R. M.
Winters, E. J.
Wiskin, J. G.
Wyllie, D. G.
Yule, D. C.

1951

Anderson, J. M.
Angus, K. M.
Armson, K. A.
Armstrong, R. H.
Austin, P. R.
Ball, G. H.
Barna, G.
Beverly, M. C.
Bocking, J. C.
Bourchier, R. J.
Brackenbury, S. B. K.
Charlesworth, W. J.

Cleaveley, W. G. L.
Collict, F. T.
Conboy, A. R.
Cooke, W. R.
Danes, A. E.
Elliott, K. R.
Fasken, W. M.
Gooderham, W. G.
Harrison, P. J.
Heeney, C. J.
Hewetson, J. H.
Hiscock, W. W.
Holmes, S. C.
Hoogen, A. H.
Irwin, J. D.
Irwin, W. A. C.
Jenns, W. E.
Keddie, J. R.
Ladell, J. L.
Lambden, J. R.
Lane, C. H.
Larke, J. R.
Logan, G. L.
Lyndon, N. P.
McKee, F. M.
McLean, M. M.
Maslen, W. G.
Masterson, P. G.
Mepham, V. A. W.
Merritt, V. G.
Morris, A. S.
Mullen, J. L.
Nozzolillo, L. J.
Paterson, L. S.
Patrick, R. B.
Peacock, H. A.
Powell, R. E.
Racey, A. G.
Seaton, H. M.
Sheldon, S. B.
Stringer, G. K.
Suter, S. R.
Ward, E. J.
White, E. J.
Williams, D. E.
Wilson, M. A.

1952
Ackehurst, D. A.
Ackerman, R. F.
Adam, M.
Beatty, W. F.
Clark, W. K.
Coats, J. D.
Coles, H. A.

Cunningham, D. L.
Cutler, D. R.
Davis, A. E.
Davis, L. C. E.
Deconkey, F. V.
deVries, H. H.
Dixon, J. M.
Dougall, A. G.
Fingland, J. A.
Fisk, V. W.
Flann, I. B.
Green, P. L.
Gregory, C. W.
Halliday, R. J.
Henry, H. J.
Higgs, K. G.
Horton, K. W.
Howe, S. C.
Hundt, A. D.
Jonas, W. E.
Keenan, J. W.
Macdonald, D. R.
McPhail, R. A.
Magnus, V. J. J.
Manning, N. K.
Price, M. B.
Scott, J. C.
Seeley, W. C.
Shannon, R. E.
Sooaru, E.
Wahl, W. W.
Ward, E. J.
Warren, G. W.
West, P. H.
Wilson, D. E.

1953
Armstrong, D. L.
Aro, R. N.
Bell, D. T.
Booth, R. W.
Chrosciewicz, Z.
Daley, J. V.
Earle, W. E.
Jefferies, J. E.
Keen, R. E.
Kristoffersen, A.
Loucks, O. L.
Nelson, R. W.
Nighswander, J. E.
Piirvee, R.
Ruddy, T. J.
Skeates, D. A.
Tomkins, L. P.
Toppin, G. L.

Van Nierop, E. T. G. M.
Waterson, P. H.
Whitcombe, G. R.
Wright, J. C.

1954
Barrett, P. H.
Briggs, R. J.
Buck, T. J.
Burgar, R. J.
Cardwell, D. B.
Carman, R. D.
Casey, K. P.
Chewpa, R.
Crosbie, D. A.
Curry, G. E.
Deacoff, G. M.
Dixon, R. V.
Dunne, A. N.
Elliott, R. J. P.
Flavelle, F. W.
Forman, W. H.
Hall, W. W.
Harris, D. G. E.
Helps, F. A.
Honeyborne, D. E.
Hooke, H. G.
Horan, G. J.
McJannet, W. D.
Markus, E.
Morison, R. W.
Motyl, F. M.
Parsons, D. G.
Perkins, J. H.
Rogers, P. M.
Ross, D. H.
Scales, L. C.
Schaefer, M.
Scully, M. J.
Waddell, J. A. G.
White, T. R.
Wilson, D. M.
Wilson, E. B.

1955
Brown, W. D. F.
Chubb, M.
Curlew, G. A.
Drysdale, D. P.
Ford, F. R.
Fullerton, W. K.
Gray, J. F. H.
Griffith, R. D.
Harris, W. G.
Honer, T. G.

APPENDIX VII 111

Keith, C. T.
Kokocinski, G. H.
McLachlan, J. A.
Pierpoint, G.
Smerlis, E.
Staley, R. N.
Stevenson, M. R.
Weetman, G. F.
Wellstead, D. H.

1956
Armstrong, R. G.
Baird, N. S.
Blight, A. G.
Buell, T. A.
Campbell, A. J.
Clarke, F. P. P.
Goldie, W. J. J.
Harrott, D. E.
Hatkoski, R. J.
Johnston, J. I.
Lunham, R. J.
McClelland, J. G.
Murray, D. J.
Paul, P. M.
Payette, G. C. J.
Richards, D. A. W.
Secker, P. W.
Soyka, S. J.
Story, D. E.
Van Nostrand, R. S.
Waldron, R. M.

1957
Anderson, H. W.
Andrew, J. M. J.
Bates, D. N.

Broeren, M. P. M.
Cannon, E. C.
Cross, B. G.
Evert, F.
Fayle, D. C. F.
Guertin, J. A.
Imada, T. F.
Iwasaki, A. R.
Kelly, E. L.
McBride, W. J.
McDonald, J. B.
McMullen, J. R.
Naylor, W. R.
Sayn-Wittgenstein, L.
Scott, R. R.
Stirajs, O.
Temple, B. F.
Tomlin, D. G.
Torrance, W. J.
White, R. R.
Wynia, A. A.
Zoltai, S. C.

1958
Boultbee, W. C. M.
Glerum, C.
Hannaford, W. A. G.
Harvey, F. R.
Jaciw, P.
Lightheart, R. G.
Managhan, W. T. J.
Newman, W. B.
Osborne, J. E.
Parks, C. R.
Petro, F. J.
Prete, L. P. P.
Prins, P. G.

Rinas, J. A.
Sadreika, V.
Sprague, C. J.
Sugden, M. J. J.
Tieman, W. D.
Van Nooten, B. A. A. J.
Wells, J. R.
Wright, E. E.

1959
Bernelot Moens, H. P.
Clemence, B. R. C.
Crombie, G. N.
Griffin, H. D.
Haas, L. J.
Kekanovich, J.
Malcomson, J. D.
Millar, M. S.
Morison, M. J.
Simpson, J. E.
Wilson, E. G.
Haavaldsrud, N. O.

1960
Copeland, J. L.
Dickson, D. A.
Gerrard, D. J.
Kiil, A. D.
McGonigal, H. J.
McHale, D. E.
Osler, E. G.
Post, L. J.
Reese, K. H.
Simpson, J. A.
Vonk, W.
Weistra, W.
Yanni, R. P.

REFERENCES

1. Advisory Committee on Reconstruction, II, Conservation and Development of Natural Resources. Final Report of the Subcommittee, September 24, 1943. King's Printer, Ottawa. 1944. Pp. 29.
2. Appreciation of Dr. Fernow's work by his former students and friends. Journal of Forestry 21, 1923 (326–32).
3. Ashley, C. A. (ed.). Reconstruction in Canada, Lectures given in the University of Toronto [including "Forest Resources" by Gordon G. Cosens]. University of Toronto Press. 1943. Pp. 148.
4. Brodie, J. A. Personal communication to the author.
5. Canadian Conservation Commission. Canadian Forestry Journal 5, 1909 (99).
6. Charter of the Royal Canadian Institute and regulations adopted at a special meeting—November 23, 1929. University of Toronto Press. 1930. Pp. 18.
7. Chesterton, G. K. What's wrong with the world? (Part I, The homelessness of man: 2. Wanted, an unpractical man) Cassell and Co. Ltd., Toronto. Sixth edition, 1910. Pp. 293.
8. Conservation the watchword. Canadian Forestry Journal 6, 1910 (51–4).
9. Delahey, W. A. Forest schools curricula and the needs of our woods operations. Forestry Chronicle 8, 1932 (29–34).
10. Dixon, R. M. Inventory maintenance procedure for the Province of Ontario. Silviculture Series Bulletin no. 1. Department of Lands and Forests, Toronto. 1960. Pp. 23.
11. Dr. Fernow receives new honours. Canadian Forestry Journal 16, 1920 (344).
12. Drummond, A. T. The need in Canada of forest engineers. Queen's Quarterly IX (4), 1902 (307–13).
13. Dwight, T. W. Forest research in eastern Canada. Illustrated Canadian Forestry Magazine, 18, 1922 (1098–9, 1158–60).
14. ——— Personal communication to the author.
15. Faculty of Applied Science and Engineering. Calendar 1958–59 (p. 18). University of Toronto Press. 1958. Pp. 169.
16. Fensom, K. G. Guardians of the forest. Varsity Graduate 3(1), 1949 (3–11).
17. Fernow, B. E. The farmers' woodlot. Twenty-fourth Annual Report of the Ontario Agricultural and Experimental Union 1902 (pp. 50–60). King's Printer, Toronto. 1903.
18. ——— The evolution of the forest. Twenty-fourth Annual Report of the Ontario Agricultural and Experimental Union 1902 (pp. 60–71). King's Printer, Toronto. 1903.

19. ——— Lectures on forestry. British Whig, Kingston, 1903. Pp. 85.
20. ——— The education of foresters (with description of forestry courses at the University of Toronto). Canadian Forestry Journal 3, 1907 (143–53).
21. ——— [Preliminary Notice]. Faculty of Forestry. University of Toronto. May 15, 1907. Pp. [3].
22. Forestry, Ontario, 1899. Annual Report of the Clerk of Forestry [Thos. Southworth] for the Province of Ontario 1899. Warwick Bros. and Rutter, Toronto. 1899. Pp. 144.
23. Forestry students in the field. Canadian Forestry Journal 6, 1910 (66–7).
24. Gilmour, J. D. Employment of forestry graduates in logging. Forestry Chronicle 9(2), 1933 (65–8).
25. Goodwin, W. L. A. school of forestry for Ontario. Queen's Quarterly X(1), 1902 (77–80).
26. ——— Forestry education for Canada [with discussion]. Report of the Fourth Annual Meeting of the Canadian Forestry Association held at Ottawa, March 5 and 6, 1903 (pp. 87–95). Govt. Printing Bureau, Ottawa. 1903.
27. Graves, H. S. and C. H. Guise. Forest education. Yale University Press, New Haven. 1932. Pp. 421.
28. Haddow, W. R. A brief historical and descriptive account of the Ontario Forest Ranger School and the University of Toronto Forest Area. 1947. Typescript. Pp. 30 + 7. Faculty of Forestry Library, University of Toronto.
29. Harty, W. Forestry education. Narrative of the steps taken to found a School of Forestry at Kingston. School of Mining and Agriculture, Kingston. Jan. 15, 1903. Pp. 8.
30. Howe, C. D. The training of a forester. Canadian Forestry Journal 16, 1920 (334–6). A Canadian forester's training. Canadian Forestry Magazine 16, 1920 (408–9). Practical training for foresters. Canadian Forestry Magazine 16, 1920 (471–2). Rewards for trained foresters in Canada. Canadian Forestry Magazine 16, 1920 (526–8).
31. ——— Forestry education. Forestry Chronicle 8, 1932 (21–7).
32. ——— The need of basic research for the solution of our forest problems. Forestry Chronicle 10, 1934 (143–50).
33. Hutt, H. L. Some Ontario forestry problems [with discussion]. Report of the Fifth Annual Meeting of the Canadian Forestry Association held at Toronto, March 10 and 11, 1904 (pp. 91–106). Govt. Printing Bureau, Ottawa. 1904.
34. Kishbaugh, W. A. practising forester's view of forestry education. Forestry Chronicle 7, 1931 (11–13).
35. Koroleff, A. Co-operation between forest schools and the industry in forest education. Forestry Chronicle 8, 1932 (5–13).

36. Loudon, James. Education in Forestry [with discussion]. Report of the Fifth Annual Meeting of the Canadian Forestry Association held at Toronto, March 10 and 11, 1904 (pp. 42–59). Govt. Printing Bureau, Ottawa. 1904.
37. McEwen, P. Forest fire protection in post-war rehabilitation [with discussion]. Forestry Chronicle 19, 1943 (24–38).
38. ——— Field experiences of undergraduate days, 1913–15. Faculty of Forestry, University of Toronto. MS. Pp. [12].
39. MacMillan, H. R. The profession and practice of forestry in Canada 1907–1957. Faculty of Forestry, University of Toronto, 1957. Pp. 15.
40. Minutes of the 25th meeting of the Canadian Society of Forest Engineers held in Montreal (Resolutions, pp. 75–6). Forestry Chronicle 10, 1934 (68–76).
41. Notes. Canadian Forestry Journal 5, 1909 (69–71).
42. Notes. Canadian Forestry Journal 5, 1909 (102–4).
43. Proceedings and Transactions of the Royal Society of Canada XII, 1894 (LXXVII).
44. Report of Senate Committee on the Faculty of Forestry, University of Toronto, 1906–1907. Pp. [8].
45. Report of the Board of Directors, Canadian Forestry Association, 1904 [with discussion]. Report of the Fifth Annual Meeting of the Canadian Forestry Association held at Toronto, March 10 and 11, 1904 (pp. 6–21). Govt. Printing Bureau, Ottawa. 1904.
46. Report of the Board of Directors, Canadian Forestry Association, 1908. Report of the Ninth Annual Meeting of the Canadian Forestry Association held at Montreal, March 12 and 13, 1908 (pp. 68–9). Imrie Printing Co. Ltd., Toronto. 1908.
47. Report of the Canadian Forestry Convention held at Ottawa, January 10, 11, and 12, 1906. Govt. Printing Bureau, Ottawa. 1906. Pp. 208.
48. Report of the First Annual Meeting of the Canadian Forestry Association held at Ottawa, March 8, 1900. Govt. Printing Bureau, Ottawa. 1900. Pp. 32.
49. Report of the Forestry Board, April 21, 1928. Department of Lands and Forests, Toronto. Mimeo. Pp. 7 + appendices.
50. Report of the Ontario Royal Commission on Forestry, 1947. King's Printer, Toronto. 1947. Pp. 196.
51. Report of the Royal Commission on the University of Toronto (Sessional Paper no. 42, 1906). King's Printer, Toronto. 1906. Pp. 268 + LX.
52. Report of Royal Commission on University Finances (Sessional Paper no. 65, 1921). Vols. I and II. King's Printer, Toronto. 1921. Pp. 31 and 160.
53. Rodgers, A. D. Bernhard Eduard Fernow—A Story of North American forestry. Princeton University Press, Princeton, N.J. 1951. Pp. 623.

54. Sisam, J. W. B. Report on Ranger Schools. Department of Lands and Forests. 1954. MS. Pp. 47 + appendix.
55. Society Affairs: The minutes of the twenty-fourth annual meeting [C.S.F.E.]. (Resolutions, p. 71.) Forestry Chronicle 8, 1932 (65–75).
56. Society Affairs: Forest Education (K. G. Fensom). Forestry Chronicle 23, 1947 (107–17).
57. Southworth, Thomas. Forestry in Ontario [with discussion]. Report of the Third Annual Meeting of the Canadian Forestry Association held at Ottawa, March 6 and 7, 1902 (pp. 23–38). Govt. Printing Bureau, Ottawa. 1902.
58. ———— Ontario's progress towards a rational forestry system. Canadian Forestry Journal 3, 1907 (157–63).
59. ———— Do we need a forestry college? Transactions of the Canadian Institute VIII, 1903–9 (97–303).
60. ———— Forest reserves and their management. Report of the Canadian Forestry Convention held at Ottawa, January 10, 11, and 12, 1906 (pp. 38–42). Govt. Printing Bureau, Ottawa. 1906.
61. Spring field work of foresters-in-training at the University of Toronto. Canadian Forestry Journal 4, 1908 (120–2).
62. The Canadian Society of Forest Engineers. Canadian Forestry Journal 4, 1908 (23–4).
63. Toronto students in Norfolk. Canadian Forestry Journal 9, 1913 (73–4).
64. The University Bill. Canadian Forestry Journal 2, 1906 (104–5).
65. Twenty-fifth Annual Report of the Ontario Agricultural and Experimental Union, 1903. King's Printer, Toronto. 1904. Pp. 76.
66. White, J. H. Forestry viewed as a profession. Illustrated Canadian Forestry Magazine 19, 1923 (15–16).
67. Zavitz, E. J. The Agricultural Forest Problem. Report of the Canadian Forestry Convention held at Ottawa, January 10, 11, and 12, 1906 (pp. 88–92). Govt. Printing Bureau, Ottawa. 1906.

www.ingramcontent.com/pod-product-compliance
Lightning Source LLC
Chambersburg PA
CBHW060454080526
44584CB00015B/1437